ON THE COURT WITH . . .

KEVIN DURANT

MATT CHRISTOPHER®

The #1 Sports Series for Kids

Text by Sam Page

LITTLE, BROWN AND COMPANY
New York   Boston

Little, Brown and Company
Hachette Book Group
1290 Avenue of the Americas, New York, NY 10104
Visit us at LBYR.com

mattchristopher.com

First Edition: September 2018

Little, Brown and Company is a division of Hachette Book Group, Inc. The
Little, Brown name and logo are trademarks of Hachette Book Group, Inc.

The publisher is not responsible for websites (or their content) that are not
owned by the publisher.

Matt Christopher® is a registered trademark of Matt Christopher Royalties, Inc.

Text written by Sam Page

Image of basketball on p. 117 copyright © Shutterstock.com/Lightspring

Library of Congress Cataloging-in-Publication Data
Names: Christopher, Matt, 1917–1997, author. | Page, Sam author.
Title: On the court with...Kevin Durant / Matt Christopher ; text by Sam Page.
Description: First edition. | New York : Little, Brown and Company, [2018] |
    Series: Matt Christopher the #1 Sports Series for Kids
Identifiers: LCCN 2018005732| ISBN 9780316486712 (trade paperback) |
    ISBN 9780316486705 (ebook) | ISBN 9780316486699 (library edition ebook)
Subjects: LCSH: Durant, Kevin, 1988– —Juvenile literature. | African American
    basketball players—Biography—Juvenile literature. | Basketball players—
    United States—Biography—Juvenile literature.
Classification: LCC GV884.D868 C47 2018 | DDC 796.323092 [B]—dc23
LC record available at https://lccn.loc.gov/2018005732

ISBNs: 978-0-316-48671-2 (pbk.), 978-0-316-48670-5 (ebook)

Printed in the United States of America

LSC-C

10 9 8 7 6 5 4 3 2 1

CONTENTS

CHAPTER ONE

★ 1988–2002 ★

HARD WORK AND TALENT

On January 2, 2012, NBA superstar Kevin Durant tweeted, "My favorite quote is 'Hard work beats talent when talent fails to work hard.' Following that has helped me reach my goals #WinFromWithin."

Unlike so many of Kevin's tweets, this one did not go viral. It has not had as many retweets as, for instance, a playful assurance that he could "destroy" Stephen Curry in H-O-R-S-E from 2009, long before he and Curry would team up on the Golden State Warriors and destroy the rest of the league.

But Kevin Durant's favorite quotation does much to explain his rise from a skinny kid from Maryland to arguably the NBA's best player. Even before he reached high school, Kevin once wrote that sentence—"Hard work beats talent when talent fails to work hard"—two hundred times. On his way to play in Charlotte, his coach, Taras "Stink" Brown, made Kevin fill the front and back of four pages of notebook paper with those ten words before he would allow him to play.

Luckily for Kevin, in addition to being hard-working, he is physically gifted. With sneakers on, the Golden State forward stands seven feet tall, eye to eye with many of the league's biggest centers. Yet he dribbles and shoots like a guard. That skill, uncommon for a forward, is the product of tire-less practice since the age of ten, something Kevin undertook with the help of four devoted adults: his mother, Wanda Durant; his grandmother Barbara Davis; and two of his early coaches, Taras Brown and Charles Craig.

Kevin Wayne Durant was born on September 29, 1988, in Suitland, Maryland, just outside of Washington, DC. Kevin does not share the last name of his parents, Wanda and Wayne Pratt, because Wayne walked out on Kevin; Wanda; and Kevin's older brother, Tony, when Kevin was not yet one year old. Until he was in high school, Kevin had only one parent. Wanda worked full-time for the US Postal Service in Washington, and dedicated herself completely to her children and to supporting Kevin's NBA dream.

That dream took time to develop, however. When

he was seven years old and already taller than the other kids his age, he played football at the local Boys & Girls Club. One time, the coaches challenged a weaker player: tackle the tall guy or get tackled by others on the team. Kevin, fearing for the smaller kid's safety, let himself get knocked over. Kevin has always been a nice, mild-mannered guy—maybe too nice for football.

At age eight, Kevin met Taras Brown at the Seat Pleasant Activity Center, a place where Kevin would end up spending much of the next decade. Brown first noticed Kevin, as most people did, because of his height. But after coaching him privately for a few years, he decided that the youngster had genuine talent.

Still, the dream didn't truly start for Kevin until a few years later, when he led his team to a tournament championship in Florida. That was when he told his mom he wanted to become an NBA player. Wanda Pratt spoke frankly to her son about the hard work it would take, and enlisted Brown to help him get started.

Kevin committed to basketball in a way most ten-year-olds would never imagine. He began practicing at the activity center with Brown as if it were a full-time job, staying there all day when he wasn't in school. And on school days, he would run there from his grandmother's house nearby and practice late into the night.

Brown set down ground rules for Kevin. He would play guard, a shooter's position. Kevin had played under the basket as a center, taking advantage of his natural height. Brown wanted him to develop as a skill player instead, so Kevin relentlessly practiced different shots: off the dribble, off screens, from behind the arc, and driving. These drills became the basis for Kevin's NBA game. He was also forbidden from playing in five-on-five pickup games. Brown believed scrimmages bred bad habits. Only through relentless drilling would Kevin develop sound fundamentals.

Brown also drilled Kevin on defense and made him run laps and do duck walks and crab walks up and down the court. Then there was Hunt's Hill, a steep incline outside the activity center that Kevin would have to run up. Sometimes Kevin's mom would increase the number of times he was supposed to run up the hill, waiting at the bottom in her car, reading a book. Brown and Wanda worked together to push Kevin toward his NBA dream. Kevin embraced the challenge.

That's not to say Kevin was a robot. He was a kid, who occasionally got sick of what his coach demanded of him. He cried sometimes. In one drill, Brown had his pupil lie on the floor with a pillow under his head and hold up a medicine ball in the shooting position. He told Kevin to hold it there for an hour. Kevin's arm began to hurt, and he left the gym and headed for his grandmother's. Brown waited for him outside. Sure enough, Kevin returned and picked up the ball. It was the only time he ever quit on Brown.

"I was never sure what that drill was for," Durant told *Sports Illustrated* in hindsight, "but I know it's those types of drills that made me who I am today."

Brown also gave him homework, which included writing out a certain saying about hard work beating talent. Kevin did his regular homework at the Seat Pleasant Activity Center, too. His grandmother would bring him meals, which he would eat there. He even took naps behind a curtain in the gym. Kevin had developed a training schedule too demanding for most adults, all before he became a teenager.

While Brown helped Kevin get ready for games, Charles "Big Chucky" Craig put Kevin on the court. He gave the lanky kid his first shot at organized basketball when Kevin was eight, and coached Kevin until he was fourteen. Craig encouraged Kevin and supported him, buying him food and driving him places. He'd take Kevin places a dad would, like to the movies or to basketball games. Kevin felt loyal to Craig.

"He told me to go out there and play like a superstar, and that's what I tried to do," Kevin would later recount on ESPN.

Craig told Kevin that both of them would be sitting backstage at the NBA draft one day, waiting for Kevin's name to be called. Even when Kevin himself didn't fully believe in his NBA dream, Craig projected confidence. He had a vision for Kevin's future that would eventually come true.

Then, when Kevin was a junior in high school, he received news that he thought was a bad joke. Craig had died in a shooting. He was just thirty-five. That's why Kevin wears the number 35 jersey: to honor Craig, to make sure Craig shares in his success, just as Kevin had always planned.

Kevin has paid similar tribute to his aunt Pearl. Pearl helped raise Kevin, constantly encouraging him. But, like Craig, she died tragically young, of lung cancer, in 2000. As an adult, Kevin has honored her with special editions of his KD signature sneakers. The KD VI Aunt Pearl shoes featured a floral pattern similar to that of a robe she liked to wear. The next edition was white and featured a strap sculpted to resemble an angel's wings. Proceeds from sales of all the various Aunt Pearl shoes have benefited cancer research.

Kevin never forgot the adults who helped him achieve his NBA dream. But one person was more responsible than anyone else for Kevin's determination to succeed: Kevin Durant. While his coaches and family might have pushed him, they couldn't make him devote himself so fully to training. Kevin was mild mannered. At home, he played the role of the kid brother, getting beaten in basketball and most other games by the stronger Tony. Out of the house, his height made him stand out, and not always in a good way. Growing up, he didn't have a ton of friends. His time spent in the gym couldn't have helped his social life, either. So why did he do it?

For one thing, he genuinely seemed to love the game. His mom once caught him playing with his Hot Wheels cars, but not racing them. When she asked what he was up to, he claimed to be diagramming potential basketball plays. As he got older, Kevin carried a basketball around so often that it left a series of imprints on his T-shirts.

There was also, however, the promise of a better life through basketball. Kevin spent the first decade or so without his father around and with his mother often working. There wasn't a lot of money to go around. Basketball gave him not just something to do but a chance to do something great. Sometimes he would take the train out to DC's more affluent suburbs. There, he might get in some practice, but also a glimpse of a life he could one day provide for himself and for his family.

Kevin never forgot the sacrifices of the adults who had helped him, particularly his mom's. He also never lost sight of the importance of his own hard work. One day he would give other kids what they needed to follow his path.

CHAPTER TWO

★ 2002–2006 ★

HIGH SCHOOL

Kevin Durant wanted to give up on basketball. As a freshman at National Christian Academy in Maryland, Kevin wasn't getting the ball from his teammates, and this upset him. He turned to his mom and to Coach Brown, who gave him familiar advice: work harder.

Then, before his sophomore year, something happened that would make every teammate want to pass him the rock, in high school and beyond: he grew. Kevin was always a tall kid. That summer, however, he sprouted about six inches, from six feet, one inch to six feet, seven inches. Most kids at that height would struggle to stay coordinated, but Kevin's hard work on fundamentals made it easy.

When school was out, Kevin played for the DC Blue Devils, an Amateur Athletic Union team for the best players in the Washington area. As at National Christian, however, he had flown under the radar, playing on the B-team in his first season. All that changed after his growth spurt. The coaches promoted him from a reserve spot to the starting lineup of the travel team, where he would play alongside another future NBAer, Ty Lawson.

Back at National Christian for his sophomore season, things also changed. The kid who had always been tall for his age was now tall for his sport. His long arms gave him tremendous "wingspan," a highly coveted trait in basketball prospects, as it allows them to shoot without being blocked and to block opponents' shots. Suddenly, Kevin was a star on his team—something that would remain true without interruption throughout his career. He used his height to shoot over the heads of defenders and grab rebounds. To maximize his diverse skill set, he played multiple positions. His team had the best season in school history, going 27–3.

Still, the people closest to him continued to push him, making sure he strove to get better. After one game in which he racked up a double-double (double-digit totals in two statistical categories), Kevin's mom criticized his defense, an Achilles' heel for her lanky son.

"I always let my son know I was proud of him. I

always let him know how much I loved him," Wanda Pratt would later tell the *Dallas Morning News*. "But when it came to basketball, after he would have a great game, I never let him enjoy that moment because there was something deeper he had to grasp for." Wanda knew the importance of always having a new goal in mind, and that her son could reach his full potential as long as he kept working hard to be the best.

One group Kevin did get positive feedback from was college recruiters, who became increasingly interested in the sophomore's game. NCAA basketball recruitment is a multistep process with strict rules that limit how directly coaches can contact players. First, Kevin would receive letters from plenty of schools, before visiting campuses as a junior and deciding on his eventual college.

Playing in the DC area, Kevin was close to the basketball powerhouses of the Atlantic Coast Conference, including the Duke Blue Devils and North Carolina Tar Heels. The first school to recruit him, however, was one far from the coast, and better known for its football team: the University of Texas at Austin.

Longhorns assistant coach Russell Springmann,

himself a Maryland native, first noticed Kevin as a high school freshman, when National Christian was playing at a tournament in Maryland. Springmann was not at the tournament to see Kevin, but the coach was interested by Kevin's height, even before his growth spurt, and by his shooting form, honed by hours of drills with Taras Brown. Soon after, Texas became the first college to send Kevin a recruiting letter and, eventually, was the first to formally offer him a basketball scholarship.

The prospect of a college scholarship must have been thrilling. Kevin's decision about school was far from settled, however. Really, he had two decisions to make: which college he liked, and whether he would attend college at all. While Kevin was a sophomore, LeBron James went number one to the Cleveland Cavaliers, straight out of high school. In a league in which players regularly get picked because they are tall, someone with Kevin's height and fundamentals would be desired. While Kevin, at age eighteen, would not match LeBron's physical maturity, NBA teams would undoubtedly still be interested in drafting him.

To further his basketball career, Kevin transferred

his junior year to the prestigious Oak Hill Academy in Virginia, known for its academics and its basketball dominance. Oak Hill had produced such stars as Carmelo Anthony, picked third overall by the Denver Nuggets in the LeBron draft, and then–Mavericks guard Jerry Stackhouse. There, Kevin would receive the best of everything: education, coaching, and—perhaps most remarkably—exposure. The Oak Hill Warriors played on ESPN three times during Kevin's junior year and attended all the best national tournaments. And Kevin made the most of his screen time, averaging 19.6 points and 8.8 rebounds per game for the season, with an impressive 65 percent shooting.

With exposure came offers from top schools. Both the University of North Carolina and the University of Connecticut, a Big East Conference powerhouse, were considered finalists in Kevin's recruitment. His friend and teammate Ty Lawson committed to UNC and wanted Kevin to follow him so that they could continue playing together.

Kevin was the consensus number-two prospect in the entire country, behind only a giant center from Indianapolis named Greg Oden. Kevin and Oden would be linked for years to come.

Russell Springmann worried that his team was not a front-runner. The Texas coach heard rumors of Kevin's interest in other colleges and reached out to Kevin's father, Wayne Pratt, who had recently reentered the lives of his children after reconciling with the family. Pratt, a police officer at the Library of Congress, now took it upon himself to do everything possible to support his son's dream.

"I just gave them everything I had; I mean, I emptied the tank," Pratt told the *Washington Post*. "There wasn't a place I wouldn't go; there wasn't nothing I wouldn't do. Wherever I needed to be, I would go."

One place he needed to go before his son could make his college decision was Austin, Texas. Kevin and his family never forgot that Springmann was the first to commit to Kevin, so they promised Springmann and head coach Rick Barnes a shot to win Kevin over before he decided on a school. The visit went well. Barnes and Kevin hit it off. The coach's sense of humor impressed Kevin. During the whole recruiting process, Barnes said he had a simple message for Kevin.

"I told him when we recruited him: 'You should want it all. I'm talking about the impact you can have on your sport and on other people. Look at... Michael Jordan, the great ones. There's more to it than what you see on the court. You're one of those guys,'" Barnes told *Sports Illustrated*. Barnes rightly saw Kevin as a budding superstar whose fame would be greater than that of the average NBA player.

Then, late one night, Kevin's dad called Springmann with a decision: Kevin was coming to Texas. There were many factors in his decision. Texas's strength program, led by coach Todd Wright, had an impressive track record—Kevin would need to pack on weight to survive against Division I and, eventually, NBA competition. Kevin and his father were impressed with the close relationship Barnes had with his players. And, of course, Texas's recruiting him first couldn't have hurt.

As always, however, the biggest guiding light for Kevin was the advice of his two mentors, Wanda Pratt and Taras Brown. His mom always encouraged him to be a leader, not a follower. So instead of following Ty Lawson to UNC, he led a top class of basketball recruits into football country.

"He never followed the traditional route," Brown told the Associated Press about his protégé's decision.

Before his senior season, Kevin switched schools

yet again, this time transferring to Montrose Christian School in Rockville, Maryland. With his college decision behind him, he wanted to spend one final year close to his support system in Maryland. There, he led Montrose Christian to a 20–2 season, in which he averaged 23.6 points and 10.2 rebounds per game. *USA Today* named Kevin a first-team All-America, and his team finished ranked number nine in the nation.

The highlights of Kevin's senior year included a trip to Texas for the Dallas Morning News Classic. There, University of Texas fans got to see their prized recruit up close. When one fan asked, Kevin even flashed the signature Longhorn "Hook 'em Horns" hand signal by raising his index and pinky fingers over a closed fist. The teenage basketball prodigy who had added "Longhorn" to his online screen name certainly seemed excited to move south.

And the University of Texas was excited to receive him. One of the most meaningful markers of just how much Kevin mattered to the school arrived five years later. That was when Russell Springmann, the man who first recruited Kevin, welcomed his newborn son into the world: Durant Springmann.

CHAPTER THREE

★ 2006–2007 ★

HOOK 'EM HORNS

Good game last night, and the scary thing is you're only going to get better.

Most players would be ecstatic to get an e-mail like that from a coach. Kevin Durant was not raised, though, to be satisfied. Even after a typically dominant performance, the UT freshman wanted only to get better, to work harder. So he sent Russell Springmann a simple reply: *But how was my defense?*

Kevin knew his defense would have to improve for him to reach his ultimate goal of starring in the NBA. That goal had been delayed by at least a year when the NBA changed its draft-eligibility rules the summer after Kevin's senior year not to allow any players younger than nineteen to be picked. Kevin would have to spend at least one season at Texas. Greg Oden, the only recruit ranked higher than Kevin, chose Ohio State. With those two players out of the running, the 2006 NBA draft was notoriously weak.

Even though Kevin might have otherwise taken the option of the draft to make millions in the NBA, college was good for Kevin. After just one week on campus, the slender shooter gained 10 pounds, reaching 215 on the scale. Texas's training staff achieved this transformation, in part, through one easy change: they told him to start eating breakfast (and not just his favorite food, candy).

On the court, he was the same old Kevin. Despite being a big-name five-star recruit, he treated everyone well. Later, in the lead-up to Kevin's draft day, Texas head coach Rick Barnes would tell stories about how Kevin kept score for the team trainers during a pickup game, and how he would rush onto the court with an ice pack if one of his team members got hurt.

"He's one of the guys," teammate Matt Hill told the *Austin American-Statesman*. "He's softhearted. You can tell he was brought up well."

This refrain would become common when people got to know Kevin: his mother raised him well. Unsurprisingly, Kevin got homesick and called his mom every day. She encouraged him to keep working.

And keep working he did. Texas had a young team for the 2006–2007 season. Four of the team's five starters were freshmen—the lone "veteran" of the group was sophomore guard A. J. Abrams. The work ethic Kevin brought from the Seat Pleasant Activity Center became infectious among his peers. Kevin showed up early for practices and even showed up at the gym on days when practice was canceled. Pretty soon, to the surprise of their coach, he and other rookies stayed late after practice to review film of how they played. And when the season started, Kevin showed up forty minutes before warm-ups and trained at full speed the day after road games.

They had a reason to work so hard. Despite their ages, expectations were high for the Longhorns. A poll of coaches in the Big 12 Conference picked Durant to be the conference's top freshman. Texas ranked twenty-first in the Associated Press preseason poll, despite its having lost several top players in the NBA draft—such was the Kevin Durant effect.

Thanks to the NBA's new draft-eligibility rule there was a historic level of freshman talent in Division I college basketball that season. And Kevin was the most exciting rookie of them all. Even Oden, more of an all-around player, couldn't compare to a pure scorer already listed at six feet, nine inches. Before he even suited up in a game, Kevin's legend had grown, owing to a particularly vicious dunk in practice on Craig Winder, the team's only senior.

Kevin suited up for his first game on November 9, 2006, against Alcorn State University. Texas won, 103–44, with Kevin scoring eighteen points in the first half. Kevin asserted himself over Texas's less talented opponent with no-look passes and a reverse dunk. Still, there were growing pains. Texas lost its third game of the season to Michigan State, 63–61. Kevin made just one of seven shots in the second half and Texas lost its Top 25 ranking.

Kevin bounced right back. In Texas's next game, against St. John's University in New York City's Madison Square Garden, he scored twenty-nine points and grabbed ten rebounds to lead his team to a 77–76 win. After the game, his coach said something that should have scared the rest of the country: "Kevin hasn't played well yet."

Opponents got an idea of what Coach Barnes meant in January, when Durant turned into a double-double machine. After spending his Christmas break at home in Maryland, working with Taras Brown on footwork, he started 2007 with twenty-one points and fifteen rebounds against University of Texas–Arlington. Next were thirty-seven points and sixteen rebounds in a 102–78 win over the University of Colorado-Boulder. Then he averaged thirty-three points and thirteen rebounds in three more conference games.

"He has a position," Coach Barnes told the *Kansas City Star*. "And it's all five." Texas was back in the Top 25, and Kevin was doing it all.

Kevin seemed destined to be the first freshman in NCAA history to rank in the Top 5 in both national scoring and rebounding. Still, for the player raised always to push himself, being the country's best college player at eighteen wasn't enough. He never let success distract him from the bigger picture: the NBA superstar he wanted to become.

"I could have played much better, man," he told *Sports Illustrated* after thirty-four points and nine rebounds against Baylor University. "Could have rebounded more, could have played better defense. I just have to improve on my weaknesses."

Turns out he wasn't kidding. In the Longhorns' next game, against Texas Tech and broadcast on ESPN2, Kevin put on a show. His first shot came four minutes into the game, when the Red Raiders double-teamed another player, leaving Kevin open deep behind the line. An opponent closed out, leaping to block the shot. But Kevin's long arms allowed him to simply take the shot over the hand in his face. *Swish*.

Three minutes later, after grabbing a couple of defensive rebounds, Kevin decided to take advantage of his much shorter defender by setting up closer to the basket. Before Texas Tech had time to react, Kevin caught a pass, turned to the basket, and laid it off the glass. *Swoosh!* Two possessions later, he isolated his man behind the arc and used a spin move to score off the dribble. His coach wasn't kidding about Kevin's playing every position! After just three shots, Kevin looked liked Longhorns' shooting guard, center, and point guard.

Still, Texas Tech kept up, not letting Kevin dominate the game. After the first half, the Longhorns' star had thirteen points but his team was trailing, 42–38. Three minutes after halftime, with the score now tied, Kevin secured a loose ball under the net and flushed down an emphatic one-handed dunk. He had found yet another way to score, and the Longhorns were now leading.

Not only did the 'Horns outscore the Raiders in

the second half, but *Kevin alone* outscored them in that span, 24–22. His teammates kept finding him behind the line, and he kept sinking threes. He hit from everywhere, occasionally beating his chest, a nod to the tattoo of his mother's name he had gotten inked over his heart. Meanwhile, he cleaned the glass, setting a Texas freshman record with eighteen rebounds well before the game was over.

He capped the performance by using his long arms to pick off a pass on defense, then flushing down an alley-oop dunk on the ensuing two-on-one.

"Can we just tack on another five more minutes, so we can watch this, please?" asked the play-by-play announcer.

His final stat line looked like a typo: thirty-seven points, twenty-three rebounds, five three-pointers, and three steals. Kevin's thirteenth double-double of the season tied a Big 12 record. And he did that all despite having twisted his ankle during the game.

"He's a once-in-a-lifetime guy," Barnes said.

After a couple of tough losses to start February, Texas finished its season with six wins in a row—including a double-overtime victory against number-seven Texas A&M—before losing to number-three Kansas, 86–90. Kevin was a serious candidate for national player of the year, and people were starting to take notice.

"I love what the kid is doing," Nuggets star Carmelo Anthony told the *Denver Post*. "He's a hard worker, an all-around player. He can give you everything: rebounds, blocked shots. He can score whenever he wants. He can put the ball on the floor like a guard. He has all the pluses."

Carmelo's opinion mattered. A pure scorer like Kevin, he had played just one season for Syracuse University, but had led them to an NCAA Championship. As a freshman in high school, Kevin had watched Carmelo's March Madness run with his mom. She told Kevin he might be able to do the same thing one day. Now it seemed possible. Texas was far from the best team in the country, but Kevin gave them a chance against anyone. Going from freshman champion to top-three NBA draft pick in the same year, as Carmelo had, would be a dream outcome for Kevin.

First, however, came the Big 12 tournament. Texas drew Baylor University in its first game, and Kevin, coming off an injury in that last regular-season game against Kansas, struggled. He missed his first twelve shots and, at one point, Texas trailed by twenty points. Despite not making a single basket until the final minute of the first half, however, Kevin finished with twenty-nine points and thirteen rebounds, leading a historic comeback, with Texas winning 74–69. In that one game, Kevin demonstrated how dangerous he had made Texas—and how much the team depended on him.

Texas's next game was against Oklahoma State, a team Texas had lost to in triple overtime during the regular season and had later beat 83–54 in one of Kevin's thirty-point games and the team's signature wins. Texas was leading at the half, but Oklahoma State rallied late, closing a double-digit Texas lead and tying the game at 61 with 1:26 on the clock.

On the ensuing possession, Texas's D. J. Augustin missed a shot, but the rebound was tipped out to Kevin, who was at the top of the key behind the three-point line. He threw up a shot with forty-six seconds left. In! The Longhorns were going to play for the Big 12 Championship, and Kevin had found his groove as a clutch playoff performer.

In the conference championship game against number-two University of Kansas, number-fifteen Texas looked well on its way to its first Big 12 tournament title. The Longhorns led 32–10 in the first half, behind Kevin's scoring. Then, in a repeat of the final game of the regular season, Kansas engineered a comeback. They kept Kevin contained in the second half and forced overtime, in which the Jayhawks won, 88–84.

Ultimately, though, neither team dwelled too long on the outcome. They had just learned their seeding in the NCAA tournament—Kansas was a number-one seed and Texas a fourth. And Kevin had shown enough skill to scare the rest of the bracket.

"I don't want to play him again," Kansas coach Bill Self said after the game.

Texas's March Madness started in Spokane, Washington, against the number-thirteen seed New Mexico State Aggies. The game was back and forth. Texas led 47–33 early in the second half, after a 12–0 run. Then NMSU answered with its own run, pulling within one point.

Trailing, with six minutes to go, Texas then pulled away, not with any flashy displays of three-point shooting but through the fundamentals drilled into Kevin through all those hours at the Seat Pleasant Activity Center. With defenders overcompensating to stop him, Kevin focused on passing and getting to the free throw line. "I really like getting double- and triple-teamed," he would say after the game, embracing his role as a playmaker. Kevin finished the game 15–16 at the charity stripe, accounting for more than half of his twenty-seven points. Texas won easily, 79–67.

Their next opponent, the fifth-seeded University of Southern California Trojans, was determined not to let Kevin beat them. USC's coaches had one of their taller players mimic Kevin in practice so that they could get used to going up against him. They had a plan: they would give up on trying to block Kevin's shots, instead going with a smaller lineup that would make sure to keep up with him. It worked, sort of. Kevin scored thirty points, but shot 11–24 and wasn't able to hit from deep or get to the foul line. By shutting off those two key parts of his game, USC hurt Texas's ability to come back from a six-point deficit at halftime.

More important, his teammates struggled mightily. D. J. Augustin, the freshman point guard who had been so good at facilitating offense for Kevin all year, shot 1–8, had more turnovers than assists, and fouled out. After helping bring this class of freshman to Texas, Kevin tried one more time to be their leader, clapping and encouraging his teammates during time-outs.

It wasn't enough. Texas lost, 68–87. Their tournament hopes were dashed. Suddenly, Kevin faced a big decision about his future: would he leave for the NBA? He wasn't ready to answer that question immediately after his freshman season ended.

"When I know, you'll know."

CHAPTER FOUR

★ 2007 ★

THE DRAFT

The NBA fined Boston Celtics general manager Danny Ainge $30,000 for just sitting and talking with Wanda Pratt during one of her son's NCAA tournament games. Kevin had a tough choice: to stay at Texas with his friends and continue his education or to make a bunch of cash in the NBA. It takes situations like the Ainge fine, though, to understand just how much money was at stake.

Michael Jordan, NBA legend and Bobcats owner, earned his own fine for discussing Kevin in a newspaper interview. And then there were the rumors that Kobe Bryant had called Kevin on behalf of Nike to discuss a sneaker deal in the range of $30 million to $50 million—rumors that Kobe denied.

Meanwhile, Kevin began to rack up awards that most players wouldn't dream of winning even after their senior seasons. He swept the six major college basketball player of the year awards, including the prestigious John R. Wooden Award. He was the first freshman to win it and a unanimous All-America selection.

Those awards certified that Kevin had nothing left to prove at the collegiate level. But they did not change his reasons for staying. His teammates were his friends. They had unfinished business in the NCAA tournament. He genuinely enjoyed college. An old friend from back home, Ty Lawson, decided to remain at North Carolina for his sophomore season. But he understood the pressure Kevin was under, telling reporters that his friend sounded "stressed out."

Then, three weeks after getting knocked out of the NCAA tournament, Kevin called a press conference at Texas. He was leaving for the NBA. He made the announcement in the middle of a pickup game with teammates and kept his reasons simple: "I just thought it was time to go. It's been my dream for a while. I felt I was ready."

Thus began one of the all-time great basketball debates: who should go first in the draft, Kevin Durant or fellow "one-and-done" freshman Greg Oden? The two stars had been linked since their high school days, when Oden was the number one–ranked recruit in the country, and Kevin the number two. Kevin's freshman performance had closed the gap in perception between the two players, however. Although Oden's team went further in the tournament (losing in the championship game), his numbers—15.7 points and 9.6 rebounds per game—weren't as flashy as Kevin's (25.8 points per game, 11.1 rebounds).

Listed at seven feet tall and 250 pounds, Oden looked the part of an NBA player. He was a do-it-all center in the mold of David Robinson. Kevin, despite his weight training at UT, looked gangly, with his lean frame and three-foot-long arms. He also needed to improve his defense. The difference in strength became more apparent only when Kevin was rumored to have failed to bench-press 185 pounds in a predraft workout.

Amid rumblings that he was too skinny for the NBA, Coach Barnes quickly came to Kevin's defense. "If people question his strength, they're stupid," Barnes said. "If they are looking for weight lifters to come out of Texas, that's not what we're producing. There are a lot of guys who can bench-press three hundred pounds in the NBA who couldn't play dead in a cowboy movie. Kevin's the best player in the draft, period, at any position."

Besides, there is more to being a great basketball player than strength. No one doubted Kevin would train to get bigger and stronger when he reached the NBA—his work ethic was well known. He also was not a scorer with a bunch of bad habits or mechanical peculiarities that would have to be fixed by an NBA coaching staff—Taras Brown had made sure of that. Kevin could do it all with the ball in his hands. His character also impressed evaluators. The very fact that his coach came to his defense so quickly only underscored how much everyone liked him. Kevin even made the case for himself.

"I'm not a bad guy. I've never been in any trouble," Kevin said. "I'm just a nice guy who is willing to work hard. And I will do anything to win."

At least Kevin knew in which part of the country he would end up. In the NBA draft lottery, the Portland Trail Blazers nabbed the first overall pick. The Seattle SuperSonics would pick second. Kevin and Greg Oden were likely both headed to the Pacific Northwest—they just didn't know who would be where.

Wayne Pratt had nicknamed his son "Green Room" in high school because he thought Kevin would one day sit backstage at the NBA draft with the other top prospects. On the night of the 2007 draft, Kevin did just that, wearing a gray suit, surrounded by family. When Kevin signed his letter of intent to join Texas in a ceremony at Montrose Christian, he had trouble finding a suit to fit his long arms. Just one year later he looked sharp with a Texas burnt-orange tie and matching pocket square.

Really, all the pressure was on the Trail Blazers. They had infamously passed on drafting Michael Jordan with the second pick in 1984. If Durant or Oden turned out to be anything like number 23, and the Trail Blazers picked wrong, the franchise would never live it down.

Commissioner David Stern stepped to the podium: "With the first pick in the 2007 NBA draft, the Portland Trail Blazers select Greg Oden from Ohio State."

Kevin didn't seem fazed by the choice. He sat there, smiling, clapping not just for a player he would be compared to his entire life but another kid whose dream was coming true. He knew what was about to happen.

"With the second pick in the 2007 NBA draft, the Seattle SuperSonics select Kevin Durant from the University of Texas."

Kevin hugged and kissed his mom. Nine years before, he had told her about his dream to play in the NBA, and she had told him how to do it and had been there every step of the way. Now they had arrived there, together. Onstage, Kevin towered over Commissioner Stern (most players did, but Kevin's slender frame made the difference especially apparent). Meanwhile, in the greenroom, ESPN interviewed Wanda Pratt in the family's big moment.

"He told you when he was just a very little boy he wanted to be in the NBA. Kids say a lot of things when they're little, why did you believe him?" asked ESPN's Lisa Salters.

"I believed him because he had a coach here that really supported him," Wanda said. "Our family believed in him, and he continued to work hard. We just continue to support him."

Meanwhile, in his first interview as an NBA player, Kevin was asked to explain a quotation: "Hard work beats talent when talent fails to work hard."

"It means no matter how good you are, if you don't work hard, nothing will happen for you," Kevin said. "I always use that quote. I instilled it in myself: no matter how good I am, I've got to keep working."

So he went right back to work.

CHAPTER FIVE

★ 2007–2008 ★

THE SONICS

"Hey, Kevin."

Phoenix Suns point guard Steve Nash casually said that to the SuperSonics rookie before they faced off in Seattle's second game of the season. Kevin couldn't believe the NBA legend knew his name. He was constantly having moments like this one, reminding him that he couldn't just fly under the radar during his first NBA season.

After all, the fans in Seattle invested more hope in Kevin than even the typical star prospect joining the bad team. The franchise had recently failed to work out a deal with the city to build a new arena. As a result, Clay Bennett, the team's new owner and a man with no ties to the region, had set an October 31 deadline to come to terms, after which time he would look into moving the Sonics to a new city.

The team had played forty seasons in Seattle and had won a championship there. In the 1990s, the SuperSonics, led by Gary Payton, had gone toe-to-toe with Michael Jordan's Bulls. The fans needed something dramatic to happen. During the off-season in which Kevin arrived, however, the team had also traded away its only two existing stars: Ray Allen and Rashard Lewis. Kevin seemed like the only hope.

"I don't want to put pressure on, Kevin, but I think you will save the Sonics," said Slick Watts, a former Sonics guard from the 1970s, when introducing Kevin to the fans at an event. "I think you will help keep them in Seattle."

All Kevin could do was smile politely. It was a major burden to place on anyone, much less a rookie. After all, what could he really do? The fate of the SuperSonics rested on whether or not the local government decided to fork over hundreds of millions of dollars for a new arena. No number of points from Kevin would facilitate that deal.

Points didn't come easy for him at first, anyway. Kevin made his debut in an NBA Summer League game against the Mavericks. He missed his first five shots, and had one blocked. He ended up with eighteen points on a 5–17 shooting performance in a 66–77 loss. Many Sonics games that season would follow this script: Kevin would score plenty of points through sheer volume of shots while his team lost.

Kevin's work ethic and team-first mentality never flagged. On the Sonics' Summer League team, he treated everyone as an equal. Many of those players, however, would likely never make the NBA. Kevin, meanwhile, signed endorsement deals with Nike, Gatorade, and EA Sports, reportedly worth a combined $80 million.

Newfound wealth changed little for Kevin. He kept working hard. And his mom moved to Seattle to live with him in a rental house. Wanda needed to make sure her son kept eating something more than his beloved Starburst candy now that he didn't have a college cafeteria to visit! Plus, at nineteen years old, Kevin was still relatively young, and having family close by made life easier.

Kevin played his first NBA game on October 31, 2007, against the Denver Nuggets. On the way into the arena, a security guard stopped Kevin to search

his backpack (this simple grade-school accessory would become a trademark for Kevin, even as he became more recognizable to security guards).

On the court, the Nuggets crushed the Sonics, 120–103. Kevin scored eighteen points on a 7–22 shooting performance. He also made a nice play on defense, using his reach to block of a shot from one of his idols, Carmelo Anthony. After the game, the reporters all surrounded Kevin—for the rest of the season there would be only two stories surrounding the Sonics: the team's potential move and its star rookie. He then went from the dressing room back into the arena to meet his parents, who congratulated him on a good first game.

The one positive of Seattle trading all their best players before the season was that Kevin would get ample chances to shoot the ball. New head coach P. J. Carlesimo knew his job was to build for the future, and the future of the franchise was Kevin Durant. For better or worse, the offense would run through a skinny nineteen-year-old from DC.

That playing time allowed Kevin to amass plenty of points in awful losses. Kevin averaged 19.5 points per game, shooting just 39.5 percent, as his team

started the season an abysmal 2–14 and were winless at home. After playing small forward at Texas, where he was expected to do everything, Kevin switched to shooting guard in Seattle, where he was expected to focus mostly on shooting while the other aspects of his game developed. This freedom—combined with Greg Oden missing the entire season after knee surgery—made Kevin the favorite to win NBA Rookie of the Year Award.

In between discouraging losses, Kevin gave the basketball world a preview of his future superstardom. On November 30, he scored thirty-five points against Indiana in a 95–93 win at home. He matched that career high a week later with another thirty-five points against Milwaukee, a game in which he also had eight rebounds and five blocked shots.

Even though it seemed very likely to be Kevin's only season in Seattle, he used his position as the team's star to give back to the local community. Around Christmastime, he took twenty-six kids who attended First Place, a local school that helped children from homeless families, out to buy presents and eat dinner.

"I felt like a parent," said Kevin, still just a teenager himself. "I used to do the same thing with my

mom and my brother and my father. It's something I cannot describe."

On the Sonics, Kevin became particularly close to fellow rookie Jeff Green and veteran center Kurt Thomas. After just two months playing on the same team, the thirty-five-year-old Thomas paid Kevin a familiar compliment.

"He's very humble," Thomas told the *New York Times*. "You can tell his parents did an outstanding job raising him."

Thomas could mentor Kevin in certain aspects of the game. But he was never a top scorer and, at that point in his career, was mainly a defensive specialist used to protect the paint. Meanwhile, Ray Allen, now a member of a Celtics superteam, complained that Seattle traded him and Rashard Lewis when they could be helping Kevin ease into the game and creating easier shots for the rookie.

Kevin, for his part, claimed he liked the trial by fire. For someone so focused on winning at Texas, however, all the losing could not have been fun. The entire season with the Sonics was basically a series of losing streaks bookended by promising performances from Kevin. After New Year's Day, it took the Sonics nearly the entire month to win a game.

They lost thirteen straight, during which Durant shot just 37.9 percent.

With offensive responsibility also came defensive responsibility. Kevin matched up with some of the game's most skilled stars.

"Man, I've come a long way," Durant told the *Austin American-Statesman*. "Last year coach [Barnes] said I was the worst defender he'd ever had. Now I'm guarding Steve Nash. I'm flattered."

After two home games in late January in which Kevin shot a combined 12–41, a story ran in the local newspaper, questioning whether the offense should really center around him. Those two games represented the team's thirteenth and fourteenth losses in a row. Veterans were reportedly unhappy that Kevin took so many of the team's shots, while people outside the team questioned whether he was really improving at all. Kevin took responsibility for missing open looks and promised to work harder.

The next game, Kevin responded by leading his team to an upset victory over the defending champions, the San Antonio Spurs. Kevin scored twenty-six points and, with thirty-two seconds left on the clock, scored the game-winning basket off a screen from Thomas. With the losing streak behind him,

Kevin would shoot 46.8 percent for the remainder of the season, averaging 21.4 points in thirty-seven games.

More publicity for Kevin, however, meant more criticism. As the Rookie of the Year buzz increased, some suggested that a well-rounded player on a better team, like the Hawks' Al Horford, should win instead. Hall of Famer Charles Barkley called Kevin "one dimensional," a characterization Kevin fought back against in the press, again pointing to the quality of the players he was asked to guard.

Kevin solidified his case for Rookie of the Year in the final game of the season, in Oakland, against the Golden State Warriors. With his grandmother in the stands watching, Kevin scored a career-high forty-two points and grabbed thirteen rebounds. He finished the season averaging 20.3 points per game, making him just the third teenager to break the twenty-point plateau. He led all rookies in scoring.

A few weeks after the regular season ended, Kevin's mom woke him up, screaming. He had been named Rookie of the Year. Kevin was happy to hear the news. Then he went back to sleep. There was more work ahead.

CHAPTER SIX

★ 2008–2009 ★

WELCOME TO OKC

Kevin Durant ordered a pair of Nikes—with overnight delivery. The rising NBA sophomore had not planned to play in his team's Summer League games, which are mostly for the benefit of rookies and others trying out for the team. After sitting out their first contest, however, he decided he had no interest in being a spectator. So he had his sneakers mailed to him in advance of a July 8, 2008, matchup against the Orlando Magic.

Who could blame him? A lot had changed in the three months since he had won Rookie of the Year as a member of the Seattle SuperSonics. The team had successfully relocated to the much smaller Oklahoma City. As part of the deal that allowed the franchise to break its lease in Seattle, the franchise had to pay the Emerald City $45 million up front and never again use the SuperSonics name or the signature green-and-yellow color scheme. Kevin now played for Oklahoma City. Their logo and nickname were yet to be announced, so he played that Summer League game against the Magic wearing a generic black jersey.

The team's last act as the Sonics, fittingly, had been to use the high NBA draft pick they had earned for being so bad in Kevin's rookie season. With the second-worst record in the league, the Sonics had a 19.9 percent chance of netting the top pick in the draft lottery. Much like in 2007, it was billed as a two-player draft, with a huge debate as to whether the University of Memphis's Derrick Rose or Kansas State's Michael Beasley should go first overall.

Unfortunately, their misfortune carried over into the off-season, and they fell to the fourth pick. There they took UCLA sophomore Russell Westbrook, an athletic guard better known for defense than for scoring. With their next pick, at twenty-four, they took another high-upside player in the six-foot-ten-inch Congolese-Spanish forward Serge Ibaka. In hindsight, general manager Sam Presti had the best draft of any team, despite his bad luck in the lottery.

No matter who the team drafted, however, those rookies would have a positive role model in Kevin

Durant. The secret to Kevin's notorious work ethic is that he genuinely wants to spend that much time working on his game. It's no wonder then that he suited up in Oklahoma City's second-ever Summer League game, scored twenty-two points, and led his team to a victory.

"He's the type of player that can't sit and watch," Russell Westbrook said after their first game together. "He wants to get out there and play as well. He's still a kid, so he wanted to play."

Russell was not being metaphorical, or calling Kevin a "kid at heart." Kevin was still only a teenager. He returned to Texas that summer to work on completing his degree (education, with a minor in social work). Kevin's mom had taught him the value of education, and he promised her he would finish college. He also spent time there training, as always. Specifically, he wanted to get stronger so that he could start to challenge NBA forwards in the low post and diversify his offensive game.

When the off-season ended, Kevin moved into a house in Oklahoma City with his mom and a cousin. Oklahoma City is about one-third the size of Seattle—one of the NBA's smallest markets. It had previously proved its ability to support a team after Hurricane Katrina, in 2005, displaced the New Orleans Hornets, who played two seasons in Oklahoma City's Ford Center. The city had embraced the Hornets, particularly star point guard Chris Paul. The Hornets had returned home to New Orleans before the previous season. The city was hungry for more basketball, and for another star—potentially Kevin—to replace Paul.

On October 29, 2008, the Oklahoma City Thunder debuted. Their name referred to the intense storms that hit Oklahoma as the center of the United States' Tornado Alley. Their team colors were blue, orange, and yellow, and the players hit the court to appropriately thunderous cheers. Unfortunately, after the excitement of the debut wore off, reality set in. The SuperSonics by any other name stank just as much. They trailed by twenty points after three quarters. Kevin scored twelve points.

In fact, the first Thunder season started even worse than the last Sonics campaign. They lost twenty-eight of their first thirty-one games. Fans started booing early. After a 1–12 start (and ten straight losses), the Thunder fired P. J. Carlesimo.

Assistant Coach Scott Brooks was promoted to interim head coach with assurances that he would at least finish the season.

One of Brooks's first acts as head coach was to move Kevin from shooting guard to small forward, the position best suited to his height and the one he had played most of his life before joining the Super-Sonics. Kevin had been put at shooting guard to protect him from stronger players. But the switch figured to improve all facets of his game—playing at forward would allow him to take more high-percentage shots closer to the basket and grab more rebounds. Defense would also be easier, as he would not have to get low to guard smaller, speedier players.

The switch paid off immediately. Against the New Orleans Hornets, Kevin scored thirty points on 68.8 percent shooting and got to the free throw line for eight shots. Even as his team struggled, Kevin played well, showing genuine improvement from his rookie season. In the same period that his team went 3–28, Kevin averaged 23.5 points per game with a much improved 46.3 percent shooting. His shot selection improved as he took more midrange shots and made a higher percentage of his threes (while attempting fewer). Brooks also demanded better defense from his young shooter. He compared Kevin's long arms to those of Inspector Gadget, a cartoon character who could extend robotic arms to extreme distances, and Brooks implored him to use his length to block shots.

As the holidays approached, Kevin and his teammates continued one good tradition from their Sonics days, taking ten lucky families from a program called Grandparents Raising Grandkids on a $1,000-each shopping spree. On the court, he helped his team get their long-awaited fourth win on December 31 against the Warriors with a great all-around performance: twenty-five points, ten rebounds, and six assists. Wins came more easily for the Thunder after that. And with more victories came increased recognition for Kevin as a genuine franchise player, not just as a young scorer on a bad team.

"Kevin Durant is a potential Hall of Fame player," said legendary Spurs coach Gregg Popovich. "He has the passion. He works at it. He's basically unstoppable. He can score so many different ways. His game will come together as pieces are added. He's just scratching the surface."

There were signs everywhere of a superstar in making. On February 9, Kevin and the Thunder faced off for the first time against the Trail Blazers' Greg Oden, technically a rookie after missing the previous season due to his injury. Despite the Trail Blazers' having a winning record entering the game, the Thunder won 102–93, with Kevin scoring thirty-one points to Oden's four.

That season marked the debut of Kevin's first signature shoe: the KD1s. The sneakers featured several references to his beginnings in Suitland, Maryland: a list of Taras Brown's drills on the left sole, a stamp for his mother, a badge for his father, even a reference to his grandmother bringing him dinner at the Seat Pleasant Activity Center.

Kevin didn't make the All-Star team in his first season in Oklahoma City, but All-Star weekend proved to be memorable for Thunder fans. Kevin and Jeff Green would face off against Russell Westbrook in the rookie challenge, which pitted the NBA's best sophomore players against its best freshmen. Before the game, Westbrook and Green engaged in plenty of trash talk. Kevin, in typical fashion, let his play do the talking. In a 122–116 win for the sophomores, he scored a whopping forty-six points, blowing away the previous record of thirty-six, set by

Amar'e Stoudemire. For a performance he punctuated with a mean reverse dunk, Kevin earned MVP honors.

His performance in the rookie game was typical of his entire February. During one ten-game stretch, he scored at least thirty points nine times, including a forty-seven-point performance against the Hornets. The hardest worker in basketball had done the only thing he knew how: worked that much harder. He approached pregame shootarounds, in which some players lollygag and try outrageous shots, with the intensity of a regular practice. And he took regular practices to the next level with workouts before and after.

Kevin finished the season with 25.3 points per game. His biggest statistical jumps were made in the categories of field-goal percentage (from 43 percent to 47.6 percent) and rebounds (from 4.4 to 6.5 per game). He finished sixth in the league in scoring and third in Most Improved Player voting. The Thunder ended up in the basement again, 23–59.

The biggest change for Kevin in year two in the NBA, however, was a close friendship he made with Russell Westbrook. Along with teammate Jeff Green, the two attended chapel before each game. KD and Russell's friendship would turn out to be one of the league's most compelling relationships for years to come, as they transformed into the NBA's foremost dynamic duo...and eventually into bitter rivals.

CHAPTER SEVEN

★ 2009–2010 ★

THE BREAKOUT

Kevin Durant stayed put. For the first time in five years, he didn't have to move between seasons. After spending just one year each at Oak Hill Academy, Montrose Christian, the University of Texas, and finally Seattle, Kevin got some much-needed stability. He settled down in "OKC," and he felt at home.

Compared with other cities with NBA teams, Oklahoma City is a low-key town. Kevin Durant, however, enjoyed the simple life. He drove a GMC Savana van (it reminded him of the van his late coach Charles Craig used to drive to tournaments) past a dog food plant on his way to practice from his house in the suburbs. When his mom moved out after his second season, two friends moved in. Neighbors brought him sweets. His newest neighbor, James Harden, a shooting guard the Thunder had just drafted third overall out of Arizona State, would come over to play video games. Kevin liked to think of himself as a Larry Bird type of player, someone who dominated on the court and led a simple life off it.

That didn't mean Kevin kept quiet throughout off-season. While hosting a basketball camp for kids in Oklahoma City, the third-year player made a bold proclamation.

"Anything less than the playoffs is a failure for us."

Kevin may have been on to something. The 2009–2010 season seemed different before the first game even started. Kevin no longer felt the butterflies in his stomach. He knew he had to be leader. And the results were immediate: the Thunder won their first game, against the Sacramento Kings, easily, 102–89.

His coach, Scott Brooks, claimed that the real difference in Kevin's game showed up in their first loss. The Thunder dropped their third game of the season to the Trail Blazers, 74–83. Kevin shot poorly, making just three out of twenty attempts. But he never panicked or changed his approach. He kept trying to score and played good-enough defense to keep the game close.

In the first twenty games of the season, the Thunder had a winning record. Kevin was averaging more than twenty-eight points per game. Suddenly, he ranked statistically among the league's best players. But he responded to whispers about a possible scoring title with his usual humility.

"You have guys like LeBron and D-Wade, Kevin Martin, Carmelo, and Kobe Bryant," Durant told the *Oklahoman*. "I'm nowhere near that company. I'm just trying to do what I need to do for Oklahoma City."

Kevin may have been too modest. ESPN put him on their "NEXT" issue cover, declaring him the up-and-coming athlete who would have the biggest impact in 2010 and beyond. From December 22 to January 2, Kevin scored thirty points in seven straight games, breaking a franchise record. His streak coincided with a five-game winning streak for the team and made him the first player to achieve the feat since LeBron James in 2007.

Pretty soon a trend emerged: Kevin would explode against an opponent and the other team's coach would praise him effusively after the game.

Boston Celtics' Doc Rivers: "He's going to lead the league in scoring very soon, and he's going to lead this team to the playoffs very soon."

The Indiana Pacers' Jim O'Brien: "He's as good of

an offensive player that there is in the league, doesn't matter, Kobe, LeBron—he's a great, great offensive player."

The Denver Nuggets' George Karl: "He's one of the best young scorers I've ever seen."

And maybe the best one, from the Miami Heat's Erik Spoelstra: "I'm glad that we don't play [the Thunder] again this year."

Kevin had arrived. One big reason for his leap to superstar status was hard work paying off on the defensive end. Coach Brooks credited Kevin for coming into the season focused on improving that aspect of his game. Good defense created more opportunities for Kevin on offense. Assistant Coach Ron Adams played a big role in keeping Kevin accountable.

"Ron doesn't teach me schemes or how to guard people," Kevin told *Sports Illustrated*. "He just gets on me and makes me feel bad."

Another reason for the breakout was Kevin's aggressiveness on the court with the ball in his hands. The threat to shoot from the perimeter was still there. But now he drove to the hoop more often, using his long arms to shield the ball from defenders and draw fouls. That season, he would end up leading the league with 840 free throw attempts—an increase of 316 from the season before.

This trend led to complaints from opponents, including Celtics star Kevin Garnett and Los Angeles Lakers coach Phil Jackson, that Kevin got star treatment from the referees. Kevin resisted this idea, claiming he earned his free throws.

In January, Kevin earned his first trip to the NBA All-Star Game, where he would score fifteen points off the bench. The announcement certified his place among the game's elite. However, Kevin used it as an opportunity to thank his teammates by buying them all new top-of-the-line headphones.

After the break, Kevin came on even stronger. On January 31, after a forty-five-point game against the Warriors, he passed LeBron in the scoring race. His 29.6 points per game trailed only Carmelo Anthony's, at 29.7. As the calendar turned to February, the crowd at the Ford Center began to chant "M-V-P" when Kevin was on the floor. And they had a legitimate case.

The Thunder won nine in a row during this stretch, entering serious playoff contention. Driving their success was their breakout small forward.

Kevin scored at least twenty-five points in twenty-two consecutive games, the best such streak since Allen Iverson nine years earlier. Kevin, ever humble, continued to deflect talk about the MVP and scoring title races, eagerly listing players he thought would overtake him. Eventually, his streak ended at twenty-eight games, making it the second-longest such run of all time, behind only Michael Jordan's.

The Thunder clinched a playoff spot on April 4, after a 121–116 win against the Mavericks. A week later, Kevin secured the scoring title with forty points against the Warriors. His 30.1 beat LeBron's 29.7. LeBron still won MVP—he had led the first-place Cavaliers not just in scoring but in assists and steals, too. But Kevin earned four first-place votes, an impressive feat, considering that LeBron was still considered the league's best all-around player on the league's best all-around team.

The Thunder finished 50–32. Their twenty-seven-win improvement from the previous season was historically good, and owed largely to Kevin's continued hard work. Unfortunately, the young Thunder drew the defending champion Lakers in the first round of the playoffs. Kevin would have to face off against his idol, Kobe Bryant.

Kevin learned some hard lessons in his first NBA playoff game. He scored twenty-four points, but on an inefficient 7–24 shooting performance. All night, the Lakers' defensive ace Ron Artest hounded Kevin, preventing him from getting in any kind of rhythm. Los Angeles won, 87–79. Kevin's coaches and teammates expressed confidence that he would bounce back in Game 2 and he did, scoring thirty-two points. His teammates shot poorly, however, and the Thunder lost, 92–95. Certainly the Thunder couldn't win without Kevin. But did they have the talent to win even with him?

In Game 3, the first home playoff game in Oklahoma City, Kevin took on still more responsibility. He led his team in scoring with twenty-nine points. He grabbed nineteen rebounds. And he guarded Kobe Bryant for the first time all series. Kobe shot just 34.5 percent with Kevin on him, and suddenly the Thunder had made it a series, winning 101–96. Russell Westbrook also started to heat up on offense. And in Game 4, the duo of Russell and KD combined for forty points as the Thunder blew out the Lakers, 110–89.

Suddenly, the story changed: the Lakers were old and slow. The Thunder were young and exciting.

TV analyst Kenny Smith declared that in three seasons, Kevin would surpass LeBron and Kobe as the league's best player. But it didn't last. Kevin shot just 10–37 in Games 5 and 6 as the more experienced Lakers ground out a series win.

Still, Kevin had made good on his preseason playoff promise. And now he had a new one.

"You hear me say championship a lot because last year I said playoffs and we made the playoffs this year," Kevin said. "I've seen that we have that talent and that work ethic to get to the championship. But chemistry is a big part of it. We just want to continue to be a group that sticks together no matter what."

CHAPTER EIGHT

★ 2010–2011 ★

RIVALRIES AND SUCCESS

Is Kevin Durant the anti–LeBron James?

That question came to the fore before the 2010–2011 season. LeBron reached free agency for the first time in his career, creating a sweepstakes. Teams around the league went to extraordinary lengths to court the NBA's king. Meanwhile, Kevin had his own contract negotiation with the Thunder, as a restricted free agent.

On the morning of July 7, 2010, Kevin tweeted that he had reached a five-year max contract extension with the Thunder that would pay him upwards of $87 million. That same day, LeBron announced that his next team would be revealed the following day on ESPN. LeBron's announcement special, *The Decision*, drew criticism for being self-important and drawn out. Fans were also mad that LeBron had decided to join Dwyane Wade and Chris Bosh on a Miami Heat superteam.

Pundits unfavorably compared LeBron's off-season to Kevin's low-key Twitter announcement and loyalty to Oklahoma City. The contrast between the two stars grew sharper a few months later, as Kevin led Team USA to a gold medal at the FIBA Basketball World Cup in Turkey, the United States' first in sixteen years. Kevin earned tournament MVP honors, scoring more points than any American in tournament history. And he did it without the help of the stars of the 2008 Olympic team, even without LeBron, who chose to sit out the tournament.

The rest of the league started to side with Kevin, too. Both Orlando's Dwight Howard and LA's Ron Artest said they ranked Kevin ahead of LeBron. And a poll of NBA GMs picked Kevin to win MVP, an award LeBron had won the previous two seasons.

Kevin didn't want to hear it. He admired LeBron. The Heat forward had mentored his Thunder counterpart since Kevin was a high school senior. They had each other's phone numbers. Kevin even defended *The Decision* and the right of the Heat stars to create a superteam.

"Everybody in the media tries to twist things up and say I'm the anti-LeBron," Kevin said. "We're two basketball players who love the game. We have the same mind-set, just trying to get better every day."

LeBron was similarly complimentary of Kevin. He spoke highly of his hard work and talent—two things both players combined better than anyone else in the league. Their incredible skill on opposing teams was why, regardless of their positive feelings about each other, the Kevin vs. LeBron era in the NBA had finally begun. Kevin had come a long way from being ranked below Greg Oden, whose career had been derailed by injuries.

During the 2009–2010 season, plenty changed for Oklahoma City. Russell Westbrook joined Kevin as the team's second superstar. He averaged 21.9 points and 8.2 assists per game, making his first All-Star team. Serge Ibaka was taller and contributed more on offense and defense. James Harden, the 2009 third-overall pick, playing off the bench, became a dangerous sixth man for the Thunder's offense. Even Kevin found a new way to score. With more and more teams collapsing in the paint to stop Kevin from driving, he started posting up under the basket. It was a testament to how much stronger Kevin had become since he had entered the league.

Some things stayed the same. Kevin led the league in scoring again. He still worked harder than anyone else, staying at practice later than any other teammate. He remained humble, still deflecting any talk that he deserved a mention among the league's MVP candidates. And he still put his teammates first. Just as he did at Texas, when he insisted that *SLAM* magazine put his teammates on the cover with him, Kevin agreed to appear on *Sports Illustrated*'s basketball preview cover only if he was pictured alongside two lesser-known teammates.

Kevin's commitment to the community continued, too. For his annual Christmas charity initiative, he chose a local organization called Citizens Caring for Children. He and 120 foster kids had a pizza party and played some basketball. He replaced the old TV at their activity center with a new flat-screen model and donated two video game consoles. Then he called the kids up one by one to give them their backpacks full of presents, which included iPods, headphones, and Nike apparel.

Kevin did want one thing to change, though. He wanted his team to go deep in the playoffs and win a championship. Behind the dynamic duo of Kevin and Russell, the team finished on top of its division for the first time since the move to Oklahoma City. It would have home-court advantage in the first round against the Denver Nuggets.

Despite Kevin's having led the league for scoring in back-to-back seasons, there was a sense that he had slipped under the radar, compared with the NBA's other big stars. He finished fifth in MVP voting. After the playoffs, however, Kevin was too good to ignore.

The Nuggets took an early lead in Game 1, and led by one point by halftime. Kevin had sixteen points through two quarters, most of which had come at the free throw line. Then, in the third quarter, he started to hit. A few into the period, he crossed up a Nuggets defender and shot a deep two-pointer. A few minutes later, with the Thunder down by three, Denver double-teamed Russell, who had scored twenty-one points in the first half. That left Kevin wide open behind the three-point line. *Swish*, tie game. Kevin was heating up.

Denver went back up by two and Kevin answered with another move in his offensive arsenal: a drive straight to the basket, complete with a made layup and a drawn foul. That bucket set up his next shot: he threatened with the dribble and then stepped back to hit a deep three. When Denver scooted ahead again, Kevin answered, hitting another long trey, this time with the defender in his face. The Oklahoma City crowd erupted. If he could hit these shots, how could they lose?

In the fourth quarter, he hit more deep shots but also posted up defenders and scored in transition. When Denver went small, Kevin just shot over their heads. He sealed the game with free throws as the crowd chanted "M-V-P"—maybe not of the regular season, but hopefully of the playoffs. Kevin had scored forty-one points. The Nuggets seemed unable to stop him.

Indeed, it took the Thunder only five games to dispatch Denver. Kevin was the leading scorer among all NBA players in the first round, with 32.4 points per game. Suddenly, no team wanted to run into Oklahoma City in the playoffs.

Next up were the Memphis Grizzlies. Though Denver clearly did not have the tools to handle Oklahoma City's stars, Memphis was a notoriously gritty and defense-oriented squad. Like OKC, they were also young, and led by point guard Mike Conley, who had been picked just two spots after Kevin in the 2007 draft.

Things started poorly. Although Kevin scored thirty-three points in Game 1 of the series, the Thunder had no answer for Memphis power forward Zach Randolph. He dominated down low, scoring thirty-four and grabbing ten rebounds. The bench bailed out the Thunder in Game 2, however, with James Harden leading the way with twenty-one points.

The Grizzlies took Game 3 in Memphis behind strong defense, before Kevin and Russell broke out for a combined seventy-five points in a triple-overtime thriller in Game 4. The next game was a blowout, with Oklahoma City winning 99–72. They seemed destined for a trip to the Western Conference finals.

In the biggest game of his young career, however, Kevin flopped. He took fourteen shots and made only three. He went 1–9 from behind the arc and made only one shot during the last forty-five minutes of the game. The next night, he couldn't sleep, tossing and turning, thinking about the chances he had let slip through his fingers. But he had one big chance to make things right: Game 7, in Oklahoma City.

The do-or-die final match of the series started like a nightmare. Kevin couldn't make a shot. But then he saw his mom, the person who had sacrificed so much to get him to that moment, dancing in the stands. He relaxed. He took over the game, scoring thirty-nine points and grabbing nine rebounds. The Thunder won easily, 105–90.

One season before, Kevin had said playoffs, and his team surprised everyone by qualifying. Now, after updating his goal to championship, he seemed ready to make good again. In the same season in which Kevin had been touted as the anti-LeBron, the two seemed destined to meet in the Finals, as Miami was tearing its way through the Eastern Conference playoff bracket.

The Western Conference finals, against the Dallas Mavericks, started similarly to the Grizzlies series. Kevin played well in a loss, scoring forty points. The Thunder clawed back with a win in Game 2, only to then lose the third game, their first in Oklahoma City. Facing the possibility of going down 1–3, Game 4, at home, became crucial.

At different moments, the game seemed well in hand. Kevin scored ten points in the first quarter. The Thunder hit their first nine shots, five of which were Kevin's. So the Mavericks switched to double teams and triple teams against him, and Kevin started to cough up the ball. He would finish with nine turnovers. He looked visibly frustrated by the lack of fouls called.

With 5:06 left in the game, the Thunder still led 99–84 after a three-pointer from Kevin. Behind the hot shooting of Dirk Nowitzki, however, the Mavericks climbed back. With the Thunder's opponents down by just three points, and with a minute to go, Kevin coughed up the ball again. The game was tied. Kevin got the ball for the last shot of the game. On an inbounds play, he received a pass, only to see a triple team running toward him. He threw up a three-pointer from well behind the line. Blocked.

In overtime, the nightmare repeated itself. With the score tied 105–105 and less than two minutes left, Jason Kidd stole the ball from Kevin and converted with a three on the other end. Kevin missed his last two three-pointers. The Thunder had completely collapsed at home.

"I feel upset because I let them down," Kevin said. "I let the city down."

Kevin was unusually standoffish and quiet after the game. He needed to have the game of his life in Game 5 in Dallas, with all the momentum going the other way. He didn't. Scoring just twenty-three points on 40 percent shooting, Kevin and his teammates came up short in the fourth quarter again.

His ultimate showdown with LeBron would have to wait...but not for long.

CHAPTER NINE

★ 2011–2012 ★

LOCKOUT

The day after the Mavericks eliminated the Thunder from the playoffs, Kevin told the media he wanted the 2011–2012 season to start immediately. Unfortunately for him, the 2011–2012 season wasn't going to start soon, or even on time. There was a strong chance it might not start at all.

The NBA was heading toward a lockout. The collective-bargaining agreement, or CBA—the contract between the players and the owners that determines issues such as who gets what share of league profits and whether there's a salary cap—was set to expire. The two sides could not come to an immediate agreement for a new CBA, and the owners canceled the preseason and all games through December.

With no starting date in sight, Kevin kept busy. He hosted a camp back in Texas. He considered going to play overseas. He even took up a Twitter follower's offer to come play flag football with a group of students at Oklahoma State University. (This

game led to a flag football challenge from LeBron—
the friendly rivalry had no off-season.)

Finally, the lockout ended, with the season scheduled to start on Christmas Day. That did not stop Kevin from playing Santa, as always. This time, he handed out shoes throughout Oklahoma City.

Kevin got a little revenge in the fourth game of the season against Dallas, hitting a three-point buzzer beater. Other highlights of that regular season included Kevin's first fifty-point game, against the Nuggets in overtime, and a forty-point, seventeen-rebound effort against the Minnesota Timberwolves in March.

The shortened regular season seemed like another big step forward for the Thunder. They finished the regular season with one of the best records in the NBA, 47–19, and entered the playoffs as the West's number-two seed, behind only the Spurs. Kevin defended his scoring title yet again while seeing an increase in rebounds and assists. The biggest reason for the team's continued improvement, however, may have been James Harden's 16.8 points per game, despite starting just two games all season. He won sixth man of the year and gave Oklahoma City one of the league's scariest B-units.

The Thunder had unfinished business to settle in the 2012 playoffs. And the standings would shake out in a way that would let them settle all their scores. In the first round, they drew the defending champion Dallas Mavericks, the beneficiaries of last season's OKC Western Conference finals collapse.

Game 1 threatened to be a repeat of previous year. Dallas's defense continued its good work against Kevin, and he shot just 37 percent from the field. With three minutes to go, the Mavs held a seven-point lead. The Thunder stormed back and tied it, 94–94. With a minute left and his team down by one, Dirk Nowitzki drew a foul on James Harden and got to the line, making both shots. Oklahoma City would get the ball back with nine seconds on the clock.

Kevin had struggled at times with his clutch shooting, even during his three scoring-title-winning seasons. His hands would shake on the sidelines during time-outs when he knew his team needed a bucket to win. With the game on the line, however, there was no one else the Thunder would trust to take the shot. Kevin took the inbounds pass from Russell and dribbled into the chest of his defender.

He drove to the free throw line and shot past two defenders with their hands in his face. The ball clanked off the front of the rim and then the backboard. *In!* The Thunder won.

The next game was similarly trying for Kevin. He shot below 30 percent. Kevin had better luck getting to the charity stripe in Game 2, however, and a strong team effort propelled the Thunder to a 102–99 win at home.

Kevin was not discouraged by his inability to hit with his shot. He spoke between games about his hard work giving him the confidence that results would follow. Coach Brooks similarly affirmed the team's commitment to run the offense through Kevin. Kevin rewarded his coach's faith. Dallas was unable to stop the Thunder with Kevin struggling, and when he broke out for thirty-one points in Game 3, they were left hopeless. Oklahoma City didn't just avenge their Western Conference finals loss. They swept the Mavs.

In the next round, the Thunder got a crack at the Los Angeles Lakers, the team that had beaten Kevin in his first-ever playoff series. Quickly, LA found out that this Thunder team was different from the one they had defeated two seasons ago. Oklahoma City had a fifteen-point lead at halftime and came out shooting in the third quarter. Russell and Kevin combined for fifty-two, and at one point, the Thunder led by as much as thirty-five. They won, 119–90.

As much as offense had dominated Game 1, defense ruled in Game 2. Again, Kevin rose to the challenge. With 108 seconds left on the game clock and the Lakers up 75–70, Kevin intercepted a Kobe Bryant pass. As play went the other way, Kevin hit the game-winning shot over Pau Gasol. His basket started a 7–0 run and the Thunder won, 77–75. Kevin was establishing himself as a clutch scorer.

After dropping Game 3 in Los Angeles, Kevin's heroics resumed the next night. The Thunder trailed by thirteen points in the fourth quarter, but they stormed back, behind Russell Westbrook's explosive scoring. Kevin then hit another game-winner, a three-pointer with 13.7 seconds left, and switched onto Kobe Bryant to play shutdown defense. In the biggest moments, Brooks trusted Kevin on both ends of the floor.

Kobe responded with forty-two points in Game 5, but OKC's team effort, which included a double-double from Kevin, proved too much for LA. The Thunder were going to back-to-back Western Conference finals. Even though he had lost to the defending champs the previous season, Kevin faced his toughest challenge yet in the Spurs, who had swept their first series.

Pretty soon, it seemed that the Spurs might run the table in the playoffs. They picked the relatively inexperienced Thunder apart in the fourth quarter of Game 1. And a fourth-quarter rally in Game 2 failed to get OKC out of a twenty-two-point hole.

The series moved to Oklahoma City on the verge of disaster. The Thunder knew they weren't going to shoot their way back into the series, not against an experienced and disciplined Spurs core that had won championships when Kevin Durant, Russell Westbrook, and James Harden were in grade school. So they responded with a strong defensive effort at home, winning 102–82. That win set the stage for the Kevin Durant show in Game 4.

The Spurs trailed by four, 82–86, with about seven minutes left in the game. And then Kevin went off. He scored right in the face of rookie defensive ace Kawhi Leonard from the top of the key. On the next possession, he cut to the paint for an easy lay-in under the basket. With 4:50 to go, he received a pass behind the arc and proceeded to bowl over veteran Tony Parker and nail a jumper in one move, getting the bucket and one. He scored again over Parker, and again over Leonard. He sealed the game with an alley-oop from Harden. The crowd erupted. The Thunder won, 109–103. Kevin had scored half of his thirty-six points in those final minutes. The Thunder had made it a series.

Kevin put on another great shooting display in Game 5, scoring twenty-seven on the road, to put the Spurs on the brink of elimination. After the game, Kevin revealed that he had been playing with a heavy heart. His uncle, Tyrone Pratt, was very sick. He dedicated the performance in his honor.

In their must-win Game 6, the Spurs came out strong, creating an eighteen-point cushion at one point just before halftime. However, Kevin refused to let the series return to San Antonio. He played the full forty-eight minutes for the first time all season. He scored thirty-four, grabbed fourteen defensive boards, and drew a key charge against Manu Ginóbili in the fourth quarter. It was the first charge call he got against an opponent all season.

"I just wanted to go out there and sacrifice my body for my team. I knew that would give us a little spark," Kevin said.

As time ran off the clock, Kevin walked over to his mom and brother and hugged them. All three started crying. Kevin was headed to the NBA Finals. He would get his shot at the King.

CHAPTER TEN

★ 2012 ★

CHALLENGING THE THRONE

Three and a half minutes into the fourth quarter of Game 1 of the NBA Finals, Thunder defensive ace Thabo Sefolosha stole the ball from Chris Bosh. He passed it to Kevin Durant, who took off down the court. With just two dribbles, the long-limbed sniper made it the length of the court and made the shot with one hand.

It was supposed to be the Heat's year. But they were in Kevin Durant's house.

When LeBron joined forces with Dwayne Wade and Chris Bosh in Miami, he famously promised multiple championships: "Not one...not two, not three, not four, not five, not six, not seven..." After one season together, however, they had not had *even* one. The Mavericks had seen to that.

So the Heat had plenty of motivation. The media framed the series as a battle to determine the league's best player—LeBron or Kevin, the guy who had twice finished second to LeBron in MVP voting.

Game 1 was in Oklahoma City, as the Thunder had a better regular season record. The Heat played a strong road game, dampening the crowd's enthusiasm early with a thirteen-point lead in the second quarter. LeBron physically dominated whoever matched up against him. Then, as they had done so many times in these playoffs, the Thunder bounced back behind Kevin's fourth-quarter heroics.

In the second half, Russell and KD combined for more points than the entire Heat team. Kevin found too many ways to score. One minute into the fourth quarter, he tipped in a missed Russell shot. Then he scored a jumper right in the face of the much shorter Dwayne Wade. He flushed down the fast-break dunk off the Sefolosha steal. To these, he would add a deep three, a powerful drive to the hoop, and some free throws. The Thunder struck first, 105–94.

But against an opponent as strong as Miami, this approach to winning wouldn't fly. The Thunder let the Heat get ahead again in Game 2; and again Kevin, Russell, and James Harden came storming back in the fourth quarter. Kevin scored twenty-six points in the second half, as he and Russell together nearly outscored the entire Heat team for the second game in a row.

Kevin looked like the same superstar he had been throughout the playoffs. With less than forty seconds on the clock, he made a three-pointer, to bring the Thunder within two. Then, on the final play of the game, still down just one basket, Kevin posted up LeBron under the net, one-on-one. With LeBron holding his arm, Kevin threw up a shot. It clanked off the rim. Kevin wanted a foul, pleading with the referee. He didn't get the call. The series would go to Miami tied.

Despite the loss, the young Thunder team was confident they could win the series. James Harden touted the Thunder as "the perfect team." After Game 3, Serge Ibaka would add, "LeBron can't play [Kevin] one-on-one."

In Game 3, the Thunder actually got out to an early lead but they had a hard time holding on to it. They maintained a double-digit lead as late as the third quarter, with 4:33 remaining on the clock. Around that time, however, Kevin picked up his fourth foul of the game and had to be benched so that he wouldn't risk fouling out of the game with six. The Heat took full advantage, and in his absence, swung the game. Even when Kevin came back in, the Thunder couldn't recover.

"[Kevin] made some big shots, gave them the lead," LeBron said after the game. "His fourth foul on D-Wade—we kind of got the momentum from there."

Late in Game 4, however, the series momentum seemed to shift in the Thunder's favor. With the game tied at 90 and six minutes left, LeBron drove hard to the basket one-on-one against Kevin, but fell suddenly under the net. With LeBron unable to get up off the floor, the Thunder outnumbered the Heat, but failed to score. A limping LeBron scored, to give the Heat the lead, but then collapsed and had to leave the game.

With trainers furiously working on LeBron's leg, Kevin scored on a signature pull-up jumper, giving the Thunder a two-point advantage. That was when LeBron checked back in, still walking gingerly. With 2:54 left on the clock, LeBron broke another tie with a deep three-point shot. The Heat would hang on to win, 104–98. Kevin had made another clutch shot. LeBron's had just been more clutch, more dramatic, more heroic.

"We're not going to give up," Kevin said. "We're going to keep fighting to the end and hopefully we can take this thing back to the crib."

The series never made it back to Oklahoma City, though. In the third quarter of Game 5, the Thunder lost all offensive rhythm. They didn't move the ball well. And the Heat took advantage of every mistake. Suddenly, the Thunder found themselves down twenty-four points entering the fourth quarter, on the road, against the best team in the NBA. Miami won, 121–106. After the game, television cameras caught Kevin in another postgame hug with his family in the tunnel to the locker room. Just like after the Spurs series, tears were shed. This time they weren't tears of happiness.

Kevin, ever gracious, praised LeBron. He even thanked the reporters present at the press conference, an unusually friendly postgame gesture from an athlete, much less one who had just lost a championship. But his first comments told the story best.

"It hurts. It hurts, man."

CHAPTER ELEVEN

★ 2012–2013 ★

50-40-90

One of the most significant moments of Kevin Durant's career had almost nothing to do with him. On October 28, 2012, the Thunder traded James Harden to the Houston Rockets in a six-player deal. It was not the kind of trade in which both teams received equal talents. With Kevin and Russell making significant money and Harden and Serge Ibaka both up for new contracts, the Thunder had a tough choice to make. They extended Ibaka for four years at $48 million. Harden, however, wanted a max contract, which would have paid him $60 million over four years.

Oklahoma City offered Harden four years and $54 million, but told him he had only an hour to accept the deal. He didn't blink. So the Thunder shipped "the Beard" to Houston, where the Rockets were happy to meet his contract demands.

Harden emerged as a breakout star and eventually as an MVP candidate on par with Kevin himself. Fans like to imagine, in hindsight, what might have been had Harden stayed, joined the starting lineup, and helped form Oklahoma City's own Big Three (to rival LeBron-Wade-Bosh), alongside Kevin and Russell. Could the Thunder have been the NBA's next big dynasty?

In the short term, however, the trade did little to derail the Thunder's emergence as a title contender. In fact, they seemed only to get better. The Lakers, after acquiring Steve Nash and Dwight Howard, were touted as the NBA's new superteam, but Los Angeles never gelled. Oklahoma City, not the City of Angels, featured the best basketball in the Western Conference.

In their fifteenth game of the season, the Thunder opened up a forty-point halftime lead over the Charlotte Bobcats before ultimately winning by forty-five. They had come a long way from their first season in Oklahoma City, when they were desperate to win by any score.

Kevin's game had come a long way since then, too. In addition to his already strong low-post game, he began handling the ball more and more. Before, if Kevin grabbed a defensive rebound, the team had to slow down as Kevin would hand the ball to Russell and Russell would inevitably pass it back to Kevin in transition. Now Kevin had the green light to go coast to coast with the ball. Pretty soon, the Thunder had the league's only seven-foot part-time point guard. Kevin logged his first-ever triple-double—with twenty-five points, thirteen rebounds, and ten assists—against the Warriors in November.

Ironically, his newfound ability to share with his teammates came with a quickness to find fault. Kevin had been Mr. Nice Guy his entire career—humble, hardworking, understated. He still exhibited those virtues. But now he did not hesitate to chew out younger teammates if they messed up. His wrath extended to opponents, too—in April, Kevin earned a $25,000 fine for a "menacing gesture" after dunking against the Warriors. He racked up twelve technical fouls during the season. He even received a scolding text from his grandmother: *Kev kev stop cussing so much*.

Part of his newfound attitude was just his being a good leader and administering tough love when appropriate. But it also reflected a feeling that his career was stuck in a loop. For all he had accomplished, Kevin's trophy case was surprisingly bare.

"I've been second my whole life," Kevin told *Sports Illustrated*. "I was the second-best player in high school. I was the second pick in the draft. I've been second in the MVP voting three times. I came in second in the Finals. I'm tired of being second. I'm not going to settle for that. I'm done with it."

Unfortunately, Kevin came in second once more, this time in the scoring race, which he had won in each of the past three seasons (he finished just behind the New York Knicks' Carmelo Anthony). He did, however, shoot 51 percent from the field, 41.6 percent from three-point range, and 90.5 percent from the free throw line, all of which made him the just the sixth player to ever join the 50-40-90 club.

The Thunder cruised through the regular season to a 60–22 record and the top seed in the West. Their first playoff series this time would pit them against an old friend: James Harden and the Houston Rockets. They rudely welcomed James back to Oklahoma with a 120–91 blowout in Game 1.

Houston quickly figured out a strategy for frustrating the Thunder, however, going small in Game 2. Down 95–97 with 2:29 to go, Russell found KD behind the line. *Swish*. The Thunder led by one. With the score unchanged one minute later, Kevin came off a pick and faked a shot, only to pull the ball back down and throw a bounce pass to Thabo

Sefolosha, all alone at three-point range. Kevin's improvements as a playmaker were evident. Oklahoma City held on to the win and took 2–0 lead in the series.

The celebration was short-lived. Two days later, the Thunder received bad news: Russell Westbrook needed surgery to fix a knee injury suffered in Game 2. He would miss the rest of the playoffs.

Kevin's leadership would be tested. He had to step up. And he did—quickly. Kevin quieted the Houston crowd with seventeen first-quarter points in Game 3 as his team took an early 39–19 lead.

Slowly, Houston climbed back into the game. Harden got hot just as the Thunder's offense sputtered. With OKC leading 97–96 with 47 seconds left in the fourth, the Rockets' Francisco Garcia hit from deep to give his team a two-point advantage.

Kevin took the ball up the court. He isolated his defender at the top of the arc, dribbled once, and heaved up a shot. The ball clanked off the back of the rim. It bounced off the front of the rim, and off the back again. *In!* Kevin's miraculous pinball shot gave the Thunder the win. Kevin suspected divine intervention.

"The Lord was with us," he said.

Houston proved to be a tough out, winning Games 4 and 5 despite Kevin's scoring a combined seventy-four points in those contests. With Russell out and James Harden playing for the other team, OKC's scoring depth couldn't compare with the previous year's Western Conference champion team. Fortunately for Kevin, his old pal James ran cold during Game 6 in Houston, making only seven of twenty-two attempts. The Thunder survived the first round. But merely surviving against the number-eight seed was not a good sign.

The Thunder's second-round adversaries, the Memphis Grizzlies, had given them trouble during the regular season, when Russell was healthy. Oklahoma City managed to win Game 1, thanks to a strong performance off the bench by Kevin Martin, Harden's replacement on the Thunder. Still, Martin was no James Harden. And rookie Reggie Jackson was no Russell Westbrook. As the series dragged on, Kevin tired. His shooting percentages dropped each game after he made 52.4 percent in a Game 2 loss: 47.4 percent, 37 percent, and finally, 23.8 percent.

In that especially tough Game 5, the Thunder fought hard to pick up their leader. They trailed in the series 3–1 and needed to win at home to force a Game 6. With Kevin not hitting all night, they trailed 80–68 with under three minutes to play. Clutch shooting from Kevin's teammates brought the game close, however. The Thunder trailed by two on the game's final possession.

They inbounded it to Kevin. He had a chance to save his team's season with a basket. A quick back-and-forth move allowed him to lose his man and break toward the net. With seven seconds left, however, he pulled up instead of driving to the hoop. He shot. He missed. The Thunder's season was over.

The player who was sick of finishing second wouldn't even get the chance. LeBron won his second title while Kevin watched from home.

CHAPTER TWELVE

★ 2013–2014 ★

FIRST, FINALLY

Fifty reporters from around the world descended on the Seat Pleasant Activity Center. They were there to learn where Kevin had come from, where he had honed his hoop skills. There, Kevin showed them the curtain he slept behind. He showed them Hunt's Hill, which he had run up countless times. He talked about his coaches Taras "Stink" Brown and Charles "Big Chucky" Craig. Kevin's mother reminisced about her basketball-obsessed son diagramming plays with his Hot Wheels cars. Kevin received the key to the city from Seat Pleasant's mayor.

The entire event had been staged to promote Kevin's new signature sneakers, the KD VI. It also served as a nice kickoff to what would be the best year of his professional career. Kevin turned twenty-five during the off-season and he had already experienced a lifetime of highs and lows. He still had plenty of time to create a lasting legacy on the court.

LeBron didn't win a title until he was twenty-seven. Michael Jordan's first ring came at age twenty-eight.

Maybe that was why Kevin arrived for training camp full of perspective and calm. The player who had spent the previous year obsessed with not finishing second again decided to relax and take the long view.

"Last year, I was obsessed with it," Kevin told the *Oklahoman*. "Like, I wasn't going to sleep because I wanted to win so bad. I was screaming at my teammates, at the refs, at the coaches. I got mad because I thought if we have a bad game here, we're not going to win a championship."

Kevin had always relished the process. Since his days at the Seat Pleasant Activity Center he had worked hard, trusting that good things would follow. After a temporary obsession with results, he entered the 2013–2014 season refocused on what had made him great in the first place.

What followed was Kevin's best season yet. Furthermore, he emerged as a triple-double threat, raising his assist totals, and started to shoot more threes in a league increasingly enthralled by the deep ball. (Golden State's Splash Brothers—Stephen Curry and Klay Thompson—experienced a breakout year that season.)

Just two games into the season, Russell Westbrook returned from his knee injury, but around Christmastime he required another surgery, which forced him to miss about half of the Thunder's regular-season games. While the Thunder weren't excited to be without their point guard, it did mean more touches for Kevin.

Kevin finished the season averaging thirty-two points per game and in the process took back his scoring crown. He was historically efficient, considering his court time: he attempted 20.8 shots per game and still averaged over 50 percent shooting. With Russell out, defenses knew to focus on Kevin. Still, he made only more plays. Kevin powered the Thunder to a 59–23 record. At last, he won NBA Most Valuable Player Award, edging out second-place finisher LeBron James.

Kevin accepted the award on May 6, 2014, at a ceremony at the Thunder practice facility. Wearing a blue suit and plastic-frame glasses, Kevin stood surrounded by his teammates, just as he did on the covers of *SLAM* and *Sports Illustrated*. Kevin stepped up to the podium with a piece of paper. It did not contain a speech, just a few words written as a bullet-pointed list: Mom, teammates, Russell, Scott Brooks.

"Wow. Wow. Thank you, guys, so much," Kevin said with a bashful smile. "I'm usually good at talking. But I'm a little nervous today."

Kevin thanked God, and television cameras showed his proud mother, Wanda, clapping in the crowd. Then he began to tell his story, talking about his childhood in Maryland and his early ambitions.

Kevin then began to thank his teammates, individually, by name. He talked about what each player meant to him, sometimes cracking jokes, sometimes fighting back tears. He thanked the organization; general manager, Sam Presti; and Scott Brooks and his coaching staff. He stopped to apologize occasionally for how much time he was taking but seemed determine to give everyone who had helped him his or her due.

Then he came back around to his family and friends, thanking his siblings, his dad, and his friends—all by name, of course. Finally, he came back to his mom, the person who had sacrificed so much to get Kevin to this moment. As Kevin began to choke up, his mom cried in the front row.

"When something good happens to you, I don't know about you guys, but I tend to look back to what brought me here. You wake me up in the middle of the night in the summer times, making me run up a hill, making me do push-ups, screaming at me from the sidelines of my games at eight or nine years old.

"We wasn't supposed to be here. You made us believe. You kept us off the street. You put clothes on our backs, food on the table. When you didn't eat, you made sure we ate. You went to sleep hungry. You sacrificed for us.

"You the real MVP," he finished, as the crowd broke into a standing ovation. Kevin clapped, too. They were clapping for Wanda. The video of his emotional speech went viral, gaining Kevin legions of new admirers.

That moment would have been a good end to Kevin's season. But he had a game to play the next day. The MVP presentation had come in the middle of the Thunder's second-round series against the Los Angeles Clippers. With Russell back at point guard, the Thunder had gotten their revenge on the Memphis Grizzlies in a seven-game first-round fight that featured four straight overtime games.

The Clippers had blown out the Thunder, 122–105, in Game 1. But after Kevin paid tribute to Russ as an "MVP-caliber player," OKC's dynamic duo combined for huge scoring displays in the next two games, both wins for OKC. In Games 4 and 5, the teams traded close home wins. Then, with the Thunder leading 3–2, Kevin played an MVP game in Los Angeles.

The Clippers jumped out to an early advantage, as Kevin had missed his first five shots. Then, in the second quarter, LA let Kevin get some open shots from three.

"Memo to all Clippers: do not leave the MVP wide open," analyst Stan Van Gundy deadpanned on the ESPN broadcast.

They didn't get the memo. Kevin got three straight easy shots from behind the arc. Suddenly, the Thunder were within five. After halftime, Kevin began attacking the basket, making lay-ins and drawing fouls. But he didn't stop taking long-range shots, either.

With the Thunder finally ahead 84–80 and with less than seven minutes on the clock, Kevin caught a pass from Russell more than a foot from the three-point line. The Clippers' Matt Barnes rushed out to get a hand up, remembering how deep Kevin had hit over him earlier. It didn't matter. Oklahoma City suddenly was leading by seven. They held on, to eliminate the Clippers. Kevin scored thirty-nine points, grabbed sixteen rebounds, and made five assists.

The Western Conference finals came down to the two best teams—Oklahoma City and San Antonio. It was a matchup many had expected in 2013, before Russell's injury. The Thunder had swept their regular season games, 4–0. But after the first two games in San Antonio, Oklahoma City was in trouble. The Thunder lost by seventeen points in Game 1 and thirty-five in Game 2. In their Game 6 win against LA, Serge Ibaka had suffered what seemed to be a season-ending leg injury. Without him, the Thunder would have trouble slowing down San Antonio's attack.

To the surprise of the fans and his teammates, Serge returned strong in Game 3, to lead the Thunder to a victory. Then, with their full lineup, Russell and Kevin combined for seventy-one points in a resounding Game 4 win. Still, the Thunder had left themselves no margin for error. When the series returned to San Antonio, the Spurs yet again won by a lopsided margin.

Once more, Kevin would find himself with the ball in his hands with his team's season on the line. At the end of a back-and-forth Game 6, the

Thunder forced overtime with two free throws by Russell Westbrook. With 19.4 seconds left in the extra period, Tim Duncan posted up down low and made a basket, to put the Spurs up by three. On the ensuing possession, OKC used a set play on a throw-in, in which Serge Ibaka set a pick to get Kevin open for a three. It worked. He had an open shot. He threw the ball up, hoping to tie the game and extend the Thunder's season. But it bounced off the front of the rim.

The Spurs advanced to the Finals, where, once again, a team other than the Thunder would beat LeBron James's Heat.

CHAPTER THIRTEEN

★ 2014–2016 ★

INJURIES AND UNDERDOGS

The season that most proved Kevin Durant's importance was not the one in which he won the MVP Award. It was the season after, the one in which he barely played.

During a preseason practice, Kevin complained about a sore foot. Doctors determined he had Jones fracture, a broken bone near the outside of the foot. Early estimates had him missing six to eight weeks after surgery, meaning Kevin would miss the first two months of season and would return with sixty games left to play.

While recovering, Kevin acted as an assistant coach, puttering around practice courts on a scooter and giving instruction. The injury also gave Kevin's mom a chance to take care of him, which he couldn't have minded.

Unsurprisingly, the hardworking reigning MVP quickly made it back onto the floor, suiting up for his first game of the season on December 2. The comeback was short-lived, however. He played just nine games before having to sit out again with a sprained ankle. By February, he was in a walking boot as his right foot started to hurt again. Then, on March 27, more than a month after Kevin's last game, the Thunder announced that Kevin needed another surgery (his third that season) and would miss the rest of the year.

Without their leader, Oklahoma City finished 45–37. As the number-nine seed in the Western Conference, they missed the playoffs for the first time in six years. The disastrous season ended with the firing of the head coach, Scott Brooks. The franchise replaced him with Billy Donovan, who had spent the past nineteen seasons at the University of Florida.

Meanwhile, Kevin worked hard to return 100 percent healthy for the 2015–2016 season. For the first time in his career, he actually had to *lose* weight. By June, he took shots flat-footed. And by August, he was back to making pronouncements.

"I feel like I'm the best player in the world."

Kevin would get his chance to prove it, as he returned for opening night 2015. Plenty had changed since the Spurs bounced the Thunder from the 2014 playoffs. LeBron had returned to Cleveland. That allowed the league's next superteam to rise: the Golden State Warriors. Behind the slick shooting of Stephen Curry, the Warriors beat LeBron to win the 2015 Finals, and returned even stronger.

Suddenly, the Thunder were no longer vying with the Spurs for supremacy in the Western Conference. There existed three tiers of contenders in the West: the Warriors, the Spurs, and everyone else. And Kevin had been pushed aside in the debate over who was the best basketball player in the world. There was a new anti-LeBron: Curry.

The Thunder had a good first season under Donovan, finishing 55–27. Kevin returned to form, averaging 28.2 points per game. Oklahoma City finished third in the conference, but a distant third. They were twelve games behind the Spurs in the final standings. And the Warriors went 73–9, breaking the single-season win record set by the 1995–1996 Chicago Bulls.

The Thunder blew away the aging Dallas Mavericks in the first round of the playoffs. After the previous year's injuries, Kevin was visibly excited to be back in the postseason. Then the real work began. First up was more or less the same Spurs team that had knocked them out in 2014. And just like in 2014,

Oklahoma City gave San Antonio the first game by losing in a blowout.

"It's over with," Kevin said after his team lost 92–124. "You move on."

The Thunder proved they had learned the lesson of 2014's Western Conference finals in Game 2, when they held on for a gritty road win, 98–97. The favored Spurs then took the series lead right back, but Kevin continued to show resilience. The now-veteran scorer dropped forty-one points on just twenty-five shots in Game 4. Kevin displayed his strength as a clutch two-way player, scoring seventeen fourth-quarter points and completely shutting down Spurs star Kawhi Leonard during the same span.

Russell followed that with his own breakout performance in Game 5: thirty-five points, eleven rebounds, nine assists. Then the Thunder finally returned the favor, blowing out the Spurs in Game 6, which they led 91–65 going into the fourth quarter.

The Thunder had knocked off a longtime foe. Still, expectations were low for a Western Conference finals matchup against the Warriors. Golden State seemed like a team of destiny. But Kevin made it perfectly clear that he wasn't satisfied just knocking off the Spurs.

"This is not our championship," he said after Game 6, looking to the games ahead.

The Warriors had lost only twice at Oracle Arena during the regular season, and not once during the playoffs. That trend seemed to continue in Game 1. The Warriors maintained a double-digit lead well into the third quarter. Behind two quick three-pointers from Russell, however, the Thunder made the game tight. Then Kevin closed the distance. As time expired in the third quarter, Kevin ran past the entire Golden State defense and made a scoop layup, bringing it to 85–88. As the fourth quarter started, he used off-ball movement to get open behind the line. *Swish*. 88–88.

Kevin added seven more points, to seal the victory. The Thunder had drawn first blood and, more important, shown that the Warriors could be defeated. As expected, the Warriors bounced back in Game 2. Their superior bench proved too much for the depth of OKC's bench. The Thunder just had to keep bouncing back.

Back home, Kevin made a statement. He and Russell got on the Warriors immediately, moving the ball brilliantly and sparking a 15–2 run. The lead expanded in the second quarter, as the Warriors began missing and Kevin got to the foul line repeatedly. The Thunder blew out the defending champions, 133–105. Suddenly, OKC looked like title contenders.

Game 4 would be pivotal. Playing at home, the Thunder could go up 3–1 and put all the pressure on the Warriors. Undoubtedly sensing their opportunity, Oklahoma City came out strong again, leading by nineteen at halftime. Stephen Curry, who had battled knee injuries early in the playoffs, shot just 30 percent. Meanwhile, six players on the Thunder scored double-digit points. The Thunder were on the verge of beating a team many had called the best ever.

Both teams played quickly in Game 5, though the Warriors, notorious for going small, seemed to benefit more. Kevin and Russell scored plenty of points, but, between them, they missed thirty-five shots. The Warriors, unsurprisingly, pulled out a win at home. The real opportunity for the Thunder lay in Game 6. They would have a chance to win on home court. If they lost, they would return to Oracle Arena, where the Warriors still had only lost three times.

At one point, to all the fans in Oklahoma City's Chesapeake Energy Arena, it really seemed that the

Thunder were headed back to the Finals four years after their first trip. The home team had a seven-point lead with five minutes to go. They had led since midway through the third. But then the Warriors started hitting.

First, Klay Thompson made a ridiculously deep shot, with Russell Westbrook right in his face, to cut the lead to four. The Thunder responded by making one free throw. Next was Curry, doubled-teamed and well behind the line. The Thunder's lead was now down to one, with four minutes left.

With three minutes to go, Kevin tried to force a pass inside. The Warriors broke out the other way, finding Curry unguarded behind the line in transition. Suddenly the game was tied, 99–99, and the Warriors had all the momentum.

With less than two minutes from the buzzer and the game still tied, OKC committed another costly turnover, this time when Russell stumbled. Thompson hit another three in transition. Then, with twenty seconds left, Stephen Curry beat Serge Ibaka one-on-one to get to the basket and seal it. The Thunder had blown a great chance to put Golden State away.

Game 7 pitted two all-time greats—Curry and

Kevin—against each other in a shoot-out. The Thunder struck first, creating an early double-digit advantage in the second period. But against the long-range shooting of Golden State, leads tended to evaporate. Midway through the third period, the Warriors' barrage of threes tied the game. In the fourth quarter, they pulled ahead with an eleven-point lead.

Still, the Thunder refused to go away. With 100 seconds to go, Kevin made a shot over the head of Klay Thompson, to cut the deficit to four. Curry responded by making three free-throw shots. Kevin came the other way, dribbling off a screen and trying a Warriors-esque deep three. It hit the back of the rim. Curry dribbled around the demoralized Thunder defense and made one last incredible shot. The Thunder's collapse was complete.

Kevin Durant's playoffs were over. Now the Kevin Durant sweepstakes began.

CHAPTER FOURTEEN

★ 2016–2017 ★

FREE AGENCY AND GOLDEN STATE

See what we're missing. We need you. Make it happen.

Golden State's Draymond Green sent that text to Kevin Durant while sitting in his locker room stall after Game 7 of the 2016 NBA Finals. After their comeback against the Thunder, the Warriors blew a 3–1 lead of their own against the Cleveland Cavaliers, ruining their perfect season.

During the 2016 off-season, Kevin became the most sought-after free agent since LeBron James. A new television deal caused the salary cap to rise dramatically from $70 million to $94 million. That gave nearly every team the means to sign the Thunder's franchise player.

Kevin had spoken in the past about spending his entire career in Oklahoma City. He appreciated life in a small market. He had even tweeted his confusion toward players who chose to simply join up with other stars on superteams. He had also, however, defended LeBron during *The Decision*. And in a league of superteams, Kevin had to wonder if he and Russell would ever be enough to win a championship.

In June and July, Kevin met with the Thunder, the Clippers, the Spurs, the Celtics, and the Heat. Each of the teams' presentations lasted hours. The Clippers' meeting lasted four hours and reportedly blew Kevin away. But fewer than twenty-four hours later, another report claimed he had informed LA they were out. Soon the analysts were all buzzing that KD's decision came down to staying with the Thunder or leaving for the Warriors, the team that had beaten them.

Really, Kevin may have always known in the back of his mind what he really wanted to do. He texted Draymond Green back that same night of Game 7: *I'm ready. Let's do this.*

Kevin's free-agency decision was controversial. Even LeBron James, in 2010, had recruited his friends and formed a wholly new superteam. Kevin had taken a team many already believed to be the most talented in NBA history and simply jumped on. Besides annoying the fans of the twenty-nine other teams, Kevin, some people thought, was going against everything he said he stood for. When he went to Texas for college, Kevin spoke of leading others, not joining up. He had talked about his happiness in Oklahoma. He loved his teammates.

But consider the move from his perspective. Despite their near upset, the Thunder were unlikely to overcome the Warriors in the foreseeable future. Switching sides gave him his best shot at beating LeBron and winning a title while he was still in his prime. Hadn't Kevin earned the right to play where he wanted? In what other field of work would someone who had mastered his craft be criticized for joining the best company in his industry?

After all, Kevin was a perfect fit for Golden State. They loved to deploy their small and speedy "Death Lineup" to overwhelm teams late in games. Draymond Green was the linchpin of this strategy, as he had the skills to play as a center or shoot from the perimeter. Similarly, Kevin was a hybrid player with the size of a power forward but the skills of a guard. The Warriors' Steve Kerr was the perfect coach to maximize Kevin's talents.

To the surprise of no one, the Warriors dominated the regular season. For the first time in his life, Kevin was not his team's primary scorer, and his point totals sagged a bit. But he contributed everything—free throws, three-pointers, rebounds, assists.

Kevin had one other new role to adjust to after his sometimes unpopular move, however: villain. And no fans booed louder than those in Oklahoma City. With Kevin gone, Russell Westbrook became Mr. Everything for the Thunder. He became the second player in NBA history to average a triple-double for an entire season: 31.6 points, 10.4 assists, and 10.7 rebounds per game. As a result, he won MVP.

On February 11, 2017, Kevin played his first game back in Oklahoma City. The fans booed their former hero when he was introduced and every time he touched the ball. After a time-out in the third quarter, Kevin and Russell talked trash to each other on the way to their respective benches, with each player shrugging his shoulders as if to say, "What are you going to do about it?" All that probably mattered to Kevin at that point was the score: 94–76. Fittingly, Russell outscored Kevin, 47–34, but the Warriors won, 130–114.

Playing in Oakland was a breeze. In the playoffs, the Warriors swept their first three playoff series against the Trail Blazers, the Jazz, and the Spurs. Most of the games weren't even close. Finally, the Warriors arrived at the Finals. Again, waiting for them was LeBron James, representing the Eastern Conference in the championship round for the seventh consecutive year.

The Warriors players who had been on the previous year's team had enough reason to want to beat the Cavs. Kevin had a new opportunity to beat LeBron and a chance not to be number two anymore. Suddenly the shoe was on the other foot, as Kevin found himself in a strikingly similar situation to LeBron's when the Heat beat the Thunder in 2012: on a superteam, in his late twenties, needing a title to cement his legacy.

Golden State blew Cleveland out in the first two games of the series in Oakland. In Game 3, though, Cleveland threatened to make it a series, and held a lead for most of the fourth quarter. With 1:22 on the clock in the fourth quarter, Kevin took the ball. The Warriors are known for their frenetic, ball-movement offense. In that crucial moment, Kevin drove to the net before hitting a step-back jumper in the paint.

Cleveland missed a three-pointer to answer. And as play came the other way, Kevin again called his own number. He dribbled to the line and simply pulled up in the face of LeBron for a three-pointer. *In!* Golden State was on the verge of going 16–0 in the playoffs.

Cleveland managed to win Game 4 at home behind a superb individual effort from LeBron James, who had a triple-double. Suddenly, the Warriors found themselves in the same position as they had in the previous season, up 3–1 against LeBron in the Finals. It was exactly for this kind of situation that Draymond Green had recruited Kevin. He was the insurance meant to prevent another collapse.

The Warriors led for most of Game 5. The Cavaliers stayed close, however, getting within three points at the beginning of the fourth quarter. Golden State needed a closer. They turned to the skinny kid who used to shake before big moments on the sidelines.

With 10:04 remaining, Kevin ran behind the line and received a pass. Cleveland's Kevin Love put a hand up, but Kevin got the shot off. *Splash*—106–98. The Cavaliers soon drew within six on a three-pointer. But on the next possession, Andre Iguodala found Kevin cutting to the hoop. He flushed it down with both hands. 110–102.

Six minutes from a championship, Kevin and Stephen Curry combined on a pick-and-roll. Kevin made a pull-up jumper with a hand in his face, 116–106. A minute later, Stephen and Kevin connected again. Kevin got the ball behind the arc but didn't shoot right away. He instead blew by his man for the easy layup, 118–106. The Warriors then started to pull away.

With 14.2 seconds left and Golden State up 129–117, Iguodala took an inbounds pass from Draymond Green. He immediately gave the ball to Kevin, who excitedly dribbled it down the floor with one first in the air as seconds ticked off the clock. His teammates began to find each other and hug. When the final whistle sounded, the guy who had held on to the ball so much as a kid that it left an imprint on his shirt simply let the ball roll away. Kevin Durant was an NBA champion.

Kevin earned Finals MVP after averaging 35.2 points in the five games. The previous year's Finals MVP, LeBron, walked straight to Kevin and they embraced.

"He's the only one I've been looking at since 2012," Kevin said after the game. "He's the one who looked me eye to eye. I told him we tied up [in head-to-head Finals wins] now, and we going to try to do this thing again."

As confetti streamed down from the Oracle Arena ceiling, someone tapped Kevin on the shoulder. It was Wanda Pratt. Kevin bent over in a shout of pure joy before grabbing his mom for a big hug. Some eighteen years since they both had committed to Kevin's basketball dream, he had reached the pinnacle of the sport.

CHAPTER FIFTEEN

★ 2017–2018 ★

BUILDING A DYNASTY

Fresh off his amazing Finals victory, Kevin did something unusual (for him): he hit pause. He rented a mansion in Los Angeles for the summer and posted a video of it, saying, "It's time for me to have a little break now." But, of course, he was still Kevin Durant, and not one to take a complete vacation. He told fans he'd be spending his summer in LA not just hanging out, but also working out and "getting better for next year."

On July 25, 2017, Kevin signed his new contract with the Warriors. He re-signed with the team for less money than he was eligible to receive, to leave enough room for the team to pay for other players who would keep the team strong.

Not only did Kevin's selflessness pay off for his team, but his hard work in the offseason paid off for his own performance. He managed to get even better in the new season. He averaged 26.4 points per game, up from the previous year's 25.1. His three-point shooting percentage improved from 37.5 percent to 41.9 percent. And he made 88.9 percent of his free throw shots, up from 87.5 percent the year before.

He started off the new year by hitting a major career milestone. On January 10, 2018, Kevin scored forty points in a game against the LA Clippers. The Warriors lost that game, 125–106, but Kevin made NBA history just before halftime by scoring his 20,000th career point. He became only the forty-fourth player in league history to reach that milestone, and the second youngest, behind only LeBron James. In fact, only five players have ever reached that milestone before their thirtieth birthday: LeBron James, Kevin Durant, Kobe Bryant, Wilt Chamberlain, and Michael Jordan. It's impressive company to be in, but Kevin barely reacted. As his accomplishment was showcased on the jumbotron and the crowd gave him a standing ovation, Kevin simply waved. Then he went back to work.

Many continued to call the Warriors the best team in the NBA, but these defending champions faced a number of challenges in the 2017–2018 season. Almost every player on the roster had to sit out for at least a few games due to injury. Steph Curry was sidelined with ankle and knee issues, including a sprained ankle that kept him on the bench for almost all of December and a knee sprain that had him off the court from March until the second round of the playoffs. Klay Thompson battled ankle sprains and knee strain, Andre Iguodala fought knee problems, and Draymond Green dealt with shoulder issues. Kevin, too, had to sit out a number of games, with ankle sprains and then a fractured rib. Even with all these injuries, Golden State ended the regular season with fifty-eight wins and twenty-four losses. But that wasn't good enough for number one. The Warriors were in unfamiliar territory going into the playoffs: second place in the Western Conference.

Led by Kevin's former Thunder teammate James Harden in a record-breaking season, the Houston Rockets were on a roll. They finished the regular season with sixty-five wins and only seventeen losses. With veteran coach Mike D'Antoni, a mix of All Star players like Harden and Chris Paul, and growing talents like Eric Gordon and P. J. Tucker, the Rockets were serious contenders for the Western Conference championship. Soon, it was time for the two conference titans to meet.

In the postseason, the Warriors breezed past the Spurs and then the Pelicans in five-game series, and the Rockets did the same in five-game series against the Timberwolves and the Jazz. The Warriors got off to a great start in Game 1, winning the game, 119–106. Kevin was his team's leading scorer, with thirty-seven points. Coach Kerr pulled Kevin late in the third quarter, after Kevin had played just over forty minutes. When asked if he'd prefer to play the entire forty-eight minutes, Kevin immediately replied that he probably would.

"This is why anybody would want him on their team," Kerr said, raving about Kevin's performance after his fourth thirty-point game of the postseason. "He can get any shot he wants."

In Game 2, Kevin was again the lead scorer, with thirty-eight points, but it wasn't enough—Golden State lost, 127–105. The Warriors answered back in Game 3, winning their first home game of the series, 126–85. But the Rockets tied the series up in Game 4 with a close 95–92 win and took another close game, 98–94. That win came at a price for Houston: Chris Paul suffered a strained hamstring in the final minutes of Game 5, which would keep him on the bench for the rest of the series. Houston would need to win Game 6 without one of their leaders, and the game was do-or-die for the Warriors.

With thirty-five points from Klay, twenty-nine from Steph, and twenty-three from Kevin, the Warriors kept their Finals hopes alive, trouncing Houston, 115–86.

The series was now tied, 3–3, and the Rockets and Warriors were each determined to make it to the Finals. Either team was strongly favored to beat Eastern Conference champions Cleveland, who had just emerged victorious from their own seven-game series against the Boston Celtics.

At halftime in Game 7, things were looking bleak for Golden State. They were down by eleven points and many observers felt they didn't have their usual energy—it looked, some commentators said, like Houston *wanted* it more. The Warriors came roaring back in the third quarter, with thirty-three points, but perhaps more critically, the Rockets came to a standstill. They managed just fifteen points in the quarter, and missed all fourteen of their three-point attempts. Houston fell apart in the second half, and the Warriors powered through to a 101–92 victory. Once again, Kevin was the leading scorer, with thirty-four points. In fact, his 213 points in the Rockets-Warriors series set a record for most by any player in a Western Conference finals. His team would go to the NBA Finals once again!

Before Golden State faced Cleveland, Kevin had to face some tough questions. The press speculated whether Kevin could really compare to LeBron, and whether Kevin could carry a team the way LeBron carried the Cavs. "I can't control that," Kevin said. "I know what I bring to my team. I know my role on my team. I'm just trying to play in a way that will help us win a championship. That's the only thing I can do."

And that's exactly what Kevin did: played in a way that helped his team win it all. Kevin delivered an especially epic performance in Game 3, where he logged a playoff career record of forty-three points, thirteen rebounds, and seven assists. Game after game, the Warriors brought their best to the court, and despite almost losing Game 1, they came back in overtime and then swept Cleveland in four games.

Kevin and his teammates were NBA champions once again! And Kevin earned another Finals MVP trophy for his incredible play. He put his new MVP trophy next to the previous year's, saying, "Reminds me of when I was a kid. My brother and I would line up all our fifth-place trophies from the rec league on the dresser and see who could stack the most."

CHAPTER SIXTEEN

★ **2018 and Beyond** ★

HARD WORK PAYS OFF

As a reigning NBA champion, Kevin Durant is not content. The debate as to who is the best player in the NBA—Kevin or LeBron—has begun anew. Kevin Durant is nobody's number two.

In fact, halfway through the 2017–2018 season, buzz began that Kevin might win Defensive Player of the Year. For a player whose defense was considered a weakness coming out of college, this possibility was amazing (ultimately, he wasn't one of the top three finalists for the honor). Despite having achieved everything a player in the NBA can achieve, he continues to work at his game.

Away from the court, Kevin has kept busy, too. He has traveled around the world and experienced other cultures. He attended Super Bowl 50...as a photographer. Kevin shot the big game from the sideline for Derek Jeter's *Players' Tribune*. In 2017, he launched a YouTube channel that quickly attracted hundreds of thousands of followers and tens of millions of views for Kevin's vlogs. He has started the

Durant Company, which invests in technology companies founded in nearby Silicon Valley. He even has an impressive collection of vintage T-shirts.

Perhaps his most important venture, however, is Build It and They Will Ball, a project funded by the Kevin Durant Charity Foundation which renovates and constructs courts for underprivileged youth both in the United States and abroad. Through the initiative, Kevin has unveiled state-of-the-art courts in places that were important on his journey—such as Seat Pleasant, Austin, Seattle, Oklahoma City, and Oakland—and places that just have a lot of kids excited to play—such as New York City; Guangzhou, China; Berlin, Germany; and Delhi, India.

"I've always wanted to play a leadership role in communities and neighborhoods—like the one I grew up in—and give kids a chance to choose health, teamwork, and basketball over some of the other negative influences they may face," said Kevin when the project was announced.

Most of the kids who step on these courts with the KD logo will not have Kevin's talent. They will all, however, have something to gain from being there. Besides, talent isn't everything. As a wise man once said: "Hard work beats talent when talent fails to work hard."

Kevin gets a rebound and makes the shot in a 2006 Texas Longhorns win against the Louisiana State University Tigers.

Bill Baptist/Getty Images

Kevin poses with his first NBA jersey following the 2007 NBA Draft on June 28, where he was selected second overall by the Seattle SuperSonics.

Almost as well-known for being a nice guy as he is for being a basketball powerhouse, Kevin often gives back. Here he is volunteering during the 2010 NBA All-Star Day of Service.

Dunking on the King! Kevin dunks ahead of LeBron James (#6) during the first game of the 2012 NBA Finals.

Kevin poses with his fellow US gold medalists (from left) Carmelo Anthony, LeBron James, and Kobe Bryant during the 2012 Olympic Games.

A viral moment—Kevin wipes away tears as he accepts his MVP award and emotionally thanks his mother for all she sacrificed to help him reach this stage.

Suited up in his Golden State Warriors jersey, Kevin battles for the ball against the Cleveland Cavaliers in Game 4 of the 2017 NBA Finals.

★ KEVIN DURANT'S ★
YEAR-TO-YEAR
HIGHLIGHTS

2005

Parade magazine All-America High School Boys Basketball Team, Second Team

2006

Co-MVP of the McDonald's All-American Games

USA Today First Team All-America

Parade magazine All-America High School Boys Basketball Team, First Team

2007

The Associated Press, NABC, USBWA, CBS and *Sporting News* Player of the Year

Adolph Rupp Trophy

Naismith Award

John R. Wooden Award

Consensus First Team All-America

Big 12 Freshman of the Year

All–Big 12 First Team

Big 12 All-Defensive Team

Big 12 Men's Basketball Tournament Player of the Year
Single-season Big 12 points record (903)
Single-season Texas rebound record (390)

2008

NBA Rookie of the Year Award
NBA All-Rookie First Team

2009

Ranked sixth in the NBA in scoring
Rising Stars Challenge game MVP

2010

FIBA gold medal
First Team All-NBA
Youngest-ever NBA scoring champion
Franchise single-season points record (2,472)
NBA All-Star

2011

First Team All-NBA
NBA scoring champion
NBA All-Star

2012
Olympic gold medal
First Team All-NBA
NBA scoring champion
NBA All-Star Game MVP
2013
50-40-90 club
First Team All-NBA
NBA All-Star
2014
NBA Most Valuable Player
First Team All-NBA
NBA scoring champion
NBA All-Star
2015
NBA All-Star

2016

Olympic gold medal

Second Team All-NBA

20-plus points in seventy-one games

NBA All-Star

2017

NBA Champion

NBA Finals MVP

Second Team All-NBA

NBA All-Star

2018

NBA Champion

NBA Finals MVP

First Team All-NBA

NBA All-Star

Scored his 20,000th career point

⋆ CHAPTER ONE ⋆

1988–1999

The Early Charlotte Years

To get a sense of Stephen Curry's NBA career, take a peek at the back of his basketball card. To get a sense of Stephen Curry's childhood, take a look at his dad's.

Dell Curry played sixteen seasons in the NBA, earning a reputation—much like his son would one day—as a deadeye three-point shooter. In the spring of 1988, however, Dell was just a twenty-three-year-old shooting guard playing his second professional season with the Cleveland Cavaliers. That explains why, on March 14, 1988, Wardell Stephen Curry II was born in Akron, Ohio, the hometown of his one-day on-court rival LeBron James. That night, Dell scored fifteen points against the Knicks at Madison Square Garden and hit the only trey he attempted—a good omen for his son.

Stephen's mother, Sonya, was herself a great athlete. A three-sport star in high school, she played volleyball at Virginia Tech, where she met Dell. Many fans make the obvious connection between Stephen's and Dell's skills on the court. (Dell ranked in the top ten in NBA three-point percentage in seven different seasons.) But in the ways he surpassed his father as a player, Stephen owes a lot to his mom.

"A lot of people say whatever defensive abilities I have, I get from her," Stephen once told a reporter. "My toughness and grittiness."

The off-season following Dell's one year with the Cavaliers, the newly formed Charlotte Hornets took him as their first pick in the 1988 expansion draft. Sonya, Dell, and baby Stephen moved to North Carolina, where they would spend the next decade. During that time, the family would see the birth of Stephen's younger brother, Seth (now a point guard for the Dallas Mavericks), and his younger sister, Sydel (a volleyball player at Elon University). In those ten years, Dell would score 9,839 points, still the most in Hornets franchise history.

Though they produced two NBA players, Stephen's parents made sure no one felt the pressure to follow in Dad's footsteps. Faith and academics always came first in their house. In fact, when Stephen was a first grader in 1995, his parents founded Christian Montessori School of Lake Norman, which Sonya still runs. There, Stephen learned with his family all around. He and Seth were in a class taught by his aunt India Adams. His grandmother, Candy Adams, was the school's cook.

With Dad playing basketball, Mom had to handle discipline at school and at home. She did not allow her kids to go to Dad's games during the week, or they would be out until eleven o'clock on a school night. She once made Stephen miss one of his own middle school games; she called her son's coach to explain that he had not washed the dishes.

When he got on the court, however, Stephen showed some of the traits that now make him an NBA superstar. At age six, he joined the Flames, his local rec center's team. With Stephen bombing from deep, they never lost. Like his dad on the Hornets, little Stephen had the ability to heat up from behind the three-point line.

The team was so good that they changed their name to the Stars and eventually advanced to the ten-and-under national championships held at Disney World in Orlando. In the tournament's title game, the Stars faced off against the Potomac Valley Blue Devils, who rallied late to take the lead. Down three points with one offensive possession left, the Stars called a time-out, during which the coach drew up a play meant to get Stephen open for a three-pointer. He got the shot off, and the defenders had to foul him to preserve their lead. Now a 90 percent free-throw shooter in the NBA who regularly leads the league in that category, he stepped to the line for three attempts. He had to make all three. The first shot missed.

"It was a moment that defined my childhood," Stephen would later tell *Sports Illustrated*. "It was all I thought about for a year. I felt I could go one of two ways afterward. I could run from that moment or I could want it again. I decided I wanted it."

Stephen played other sports, too, including baseball and football. Still, the idea of following in his father's footsteps proved irresistible, and he put hoops above the rest. Appearing with his dad in a Burger King commercial as "Dell Curry & Son," little Stephen told his dad he wanted to be a basketball player when he grew up. "Boy...that's going to take a lot of hard work and practice," Dell tells his son in the ad. "You've got to study hard, too."

"I know," Stephen replies. Turns out, he wasn't kidding.

TURN THE PAGE TO START READING ABOUT ANOTHER BASKETBALL WARRIOR

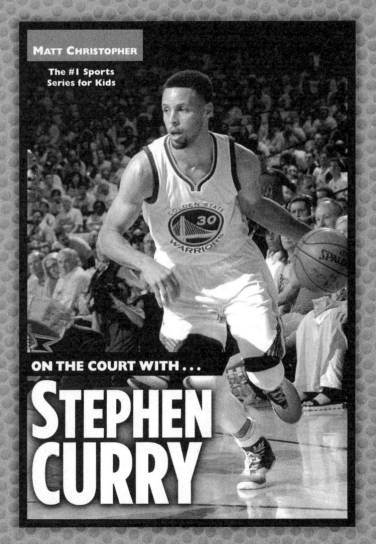